T0365316

Cambridge Elements ☰

Elements in Christian Doctrine
edited by
Rachel Muers
University of Edinburgh
Ashley Cocksworth
University of Roehampton
Simeon Zahl
University of Cambridge

LIFE AFTER DEATH
AFTER MARX

Simon Hewitt
University of Leeds

Shaftesbury Road, Cambridge CB2 8EA, United Kingdom

One Liberty Plaza, 20th Floor, New York, NY 10006, USA

477 Williamstown Road, Port Melbourne, VIC 3207, Australia

314–321, 3rd Floor, Plot 3, Splendor Forum, Jasola District Centre,
New Delhi – 110025, India

103 Penang Road, #05–06/07, Visioncrest Commercial, Singapore 238467

Cambridge University Press is part of Cambridge University Press & Assessment,
a department of the University of Cambridge.

We share the University's mission to contribute to society through the pursuit of
education, learning and research at the highest international levels of excellence.

www.cambridge.org
Information on this title: www.cambridge.org/9781009526876

DOI: 10.1017/9781009526852

When citing this work, please include a reference to the DOI 10.1017/9781009526852

First published 2025

A catalogue record for this publication is available from the British Library

ISBN 978-1-009-52687-6 Hardback
ISBN 978-1-009-52684-5 Paperback
ISSN 2977-0211 (online)
ISSN 2977-0203 (print)

Cambridge University Press & Assessment has no responsibility for the persistence
or accuracy of URLs for external or third-party internet websites referred to in this
publication and does not guarantee that any content on such websites is, or will
remain, accurate or appropriate.

For EU product safety concerns, contact us at Calle de José Abascal, 56, 1°, 28003
Madrid, Spain, or email eugpsr@cambridge.org.

Life after Death after Marx

Elements in Christian Doctrine

DOI: 10.1017/9781009526852
First published online: March 2025

Simon Hewitt
University of Leeds

Author for correspondence: Simon Hewitt, s.hewitt@leeds.ac.uk

Abstract: Karl Marx's criticism of religion, as applied to afterlife belief, needs to be taken seriously by Christian theologians. After outlining that belief, the author examines a picture of heaven implicit in much Christian belief and practice which is susceptible to that critique. He sets out an alternative eschatology, centred on the Kingdom of God and the resurrection of the body, which is somewhat less susceptible. He then explores whether a doctrine of the intermediate state can be sustained in the light of Marx's criticisms. He goes on to examine the politics of remembrance in the light of Marxist criticism, and to ask whether Christianity can help compensate for the tragic character of Marxism. A constant theme is that Christian theology should exist in tension with Marx's criticisms, never assuming that it has overcome them completely.

Keywords: Marx, eschatology, heaven, political theology, afterlife

ISBNs: 9781009526876 (HB), 9781009526845 (PB), 9781009526852 (OC)
ISSNs: 2977-0211 (online), 2977-0203 (print)

Contents

1 Introduction

You will eat, by and by
In that glorious land above the sky
Work and pray, live on hay
You'll get pie in the sky when you die (That's a lie!)

Joe Hill, 'The Preacher and the Slave'[1]

My contention is that any form of afterlife belief which reconciles people to existing exploitation or oppression is indeed a lie. In fact, for all that Christians have historically propagated views of the afterlife which do reconcile people to injustice (were this not the case, Joe Hill would hardly have needed to write the previously quoted song), I hold that *from the perspective of Christian theology* all such reconciliatory afterlife belief is to be judged inadequate and contrary to the gospel. God wills goodness and flourishing for God's creatures, not simply in some eschatological future[2] but in the here and now. Moreover, as liberation theology has taught us, God has a preferential option for the poor and oppressed, and is therefore not on the side of any doctrine which damages the poor and oppressed. Much afterlife belief, as a consequence, stands under divine judgement.

It is not my position, however, that belief in an afterlife should simply be jettisoned. Writing out of the Christian tradition, and considering myself bound by its norms,[3] I cannot simply cast to one side the hope that we will live again after death. 'If for this life only we have hoped in Christ, we are of all people most to be pitied.'[4] Yet it is immediately obvious, or should be, how this hope can become an alibi for ignoring this present world, its iniquities and its prospects. What, then, is Christian theology to say?

What is it to say *to whom*? In other words, who is the intended audience of this Element? First and foremost, since this is a work of Christian theology, I am writing for other academic theologians and for Christians more generally. But the intended range of the Element goes beyond that. I include, unsurprisingly, Marxists in the hoped-for readership. However, there are not many Marxists in the left these days – to my mind a sorry state of affairs. But there are still plenty

---

[1] Hill 1911.

[2] The distinction is sometimes made between eschatology, dealing with the final consummation of the created order, and para-eschatology, dealing with the immediate future of souls after death. I will ignore this terminological distinction here. I will, however, deal with (what gets called) para-eschatology in Section 3 on the intermediate state.

[3] Specifically, I am a Catholic and consider myself bound by that Church's *de fide* teaching. Quite how this positioning, which might to some seem entirely incongruous with the kind of liberative perspective I develop here, is to be justified is an interesting question, but not one I have space to deal with in this Element.

[4] 1 Corinthians 15:19 (New Revised Standard Version, Catholic Edition (NRSV); all biblical quotations following from this version).

of people who long for a better world in many ways: those who fight for ecological justice, for women's liberation, against homophobia and against racism, and many others. Through thinking about how afterlife beliefs cohere with, or fail to cohere with, their political practice and thought they may learn something important. In particular activists who are also Christians have a lot to gain, I think, from acknowledging and working through tensions between eschatology and political hope. But, to return to the beginning of my list, it is theologians in general I have most especially in mind. We cannot afford to ignore criticisms of eschatology, particularly when they arise out of suspicion cultivated in the name of social and political justice.

My proposal is that we can best make progress towards disentangling our doctrine of the afterlife from complicity with social wrongs by reading it critically alongside voices who, with full power, denounce religious eschatology as in some way damaging to the human condition. A lengthier treatment of this issue would certainly have to engage with the contributions of Nietzsche and Freud. Here, though, I will focus on Karl Marx. One of the most articulate and persistent critics of religion, Marx endorsed opposition to religion (including afterlife belief) in the cause of a better society. He is therefore well qualified to be a dialogue partner for present purposes.

The word 'dialogue' is important here. The point of this Element is not to criticise Marx, or to mount a defence of Christian doctrine against him. What is proposed is, rather, an uncomfortable conversation, during which we are brought, by consideration of Marx's ideas, to understand how our articulation of eschatology can become a means to escape from the struggles and suffering of our present political order – in Marxist language: an imaginary reconciliation of real contradictions. We can expect, in what follows, to learn from Marx. We can also be open to the possibility that the Marxist tradition can learn from Christian theology. We should not, though, orientate ourselves towards that possibility in an arrogant fashion in such a way as to mitigate the force of Marxist criticism of our own positions. We should not presume to take the speck out of our brother Marx's eye whilst ignoring the log in our own.[5] Reading Marx against our belief in an afterlife will, and should, prove unsettling.

For the rest of this introduction, I will very briefly provide a guide to Marx, his thought, and Christian theological engagements with that thought. After that I will conclude with a note about a particular issue in Christian eschatology. In the rest of the Element a dialogue of the sort I have alluded to will be given the stage.

---

[5] Cf. Matthew 7:4; Luke 6:41.

1.1 Karl Marx against Religion

This is not the place for a biography of Marx. The most comprehensive and readable of those remains David McLellan's (1973). It is, however, necessary to introduce the reader to the outlines of Marx's criticism of afterlife belief. This will be our constant companion in what follows. It has its context amongst Marx's criticism of religion more generally.

It is unsurprising that Marx was a critic of religion. The intellectual milieu in which he moved was one of relentless hostility to religion which was associated with social reaction and was epitomised in Hegel, as read by the 'right' Hegelians as providing a theological justification for the Prussian state. Marx initially moved in 'left' Hegelian circles.[6] These included radical biblical scholars David Strauss and Bruno Bauer, and philosopher Arnold Ruge. The left Hegelians were infamous for their attacks on religion, and suffered for them, variously losing work and standing. In due course Marx came to be critical of the left Hegelians, but their opposition to the established order of things, and to religion which upheld that established order of things, set the scene for Marx's subsequent work.

More influential still on Marx's attitude towards religion was Ludwig Feuerbach. In his *The Essence of Christianity* ([1843] 1972) Feuerbach suggests that religious concepts (and especially the concept of God) result from the projection of human nature onto an imagined divinity. In religion people encounter their own reality as something external to them. Religion is, then, a fundamental distortion of reality. Parenthetically, Karl Barth (2001, ch. 18) considered Feuerbach as part of the history of Protestant theology, his point being that it is *true* that people project their own nature onto God, and this ought to be recognised by Christian theology.

Be that as it may, Marx took up the baton from Feuerbach. He agreed that religious concepts resulted from the projection of what is authentically human (in particular the human essence, or *species-being*) onto an alien religious reality. He further held, however, that the alienation contained within religion had a social explanation. Alienation in the religious sphere, for Marx, arose from the alienation of labour, from the fact that in their everyday lives the mass of people stand in unfulfilling relations. These relations were epitomised for Marx at this stage in his work not only by the relations instanced in wage-labour but also by their relations to the state. What people cannot, in virtue of these relations, have on earth, they project onto heaven. And once projected, the resulting religious fantasies serve to reconcile the alienated to their lot.

---

[6] See McLellan 1972.

With these additional insights on board, Marx held that German thought – including especially the thinkers previously mentioned – has said what needs to be said about religion. 'The criticism of religion is the prerequisite of all criticism', writes Marx, but he also says that, 'for Germany, the criticism of religion has been essentially completed' (Marx [1844] 1970). This being so, Marx advocated turning 'the criticism of heaven . . . into the criticism of earth'. Critical and practical energy should be dedicated to understanding, and overthrowing, the capitalist order, rather than being focused on opposition to religion. This political orientation is important for the theologian who would engage with Marx to take on board. Marx thought that religious alienation is grounded in secular, this-worldly alienation, and his priority is dealing with the latter (Marx [1843] 2003). Criticism of religion can be a distraction from this task, and Marx was certainly no armchair critic of religion.

Nevertheless, Marx *was* critical of religion, in general, and of the idea of an afterlife, in particular. For Christian theology, which certainly has not taken on board the criticism of religion as had the German philosophy of the early nineteenth century, engagement with what Marx does say about religion, and about heaven, will be constructive. And in that spirit what I propose here is an attempt at dogmatic reconstruction in critical dialogue with Marx. This I take to be a legitimate task of Christian theology. We should, however, heed a Marxian warning. Religious alienation, Marx claims, results from alienation in other spheres, especially the economic. Suppose he is right. Then those beliefs concerning heaven (for instance) that we find reason to criticise from the perspective of Christian theology will have deeper roots than the merely intellectual. Attacking inadequate belief on the doctrinal plane may not be enough to bring about conversion from those beliefs. Instead, it may be through struggle against the secular basis of those beliefs that progress is made. The theologian, too, might have cause to turn the criticism of heaven into criticism of earth. A good theologian, whilst she cannot forget the intellectual task of articulating the faith anew, will – on this account – need to be an activist if her articulation is to find a hearing.

1.2 Christian Theology and Marx

Again, it is neither possible nor appropriate to provide here a survey of the vast literature on the relationship between Marx and Christian theology – attempts at dialogue, comparison, and censure. A good survey of some of these, albeit within a different framework from that adopted here, is Peter Scott's (2022). In the brief space available, however, I do want to address some treatments of relevance to the topic of this Element. These can be divided up into those which regard Marx and Marxism as sources of socio-economic insight, setting aside the critique of religion touched on earlier, and those which engage with that critique directly. After looking at these, I want to pay particular attention to the work of Nicholas Lash, which is directly salient for our purposes. Before setting about these tasks, I should note in passing that the authors examined for these purposes are exclusively male, pointing to a limitation of this area of investigation which needs to be addressed.

The best known setting for theological engagement with Marx since the mid twentieth century has been Latin American liberation theology. Although the extent of liberation theology's dependence on Marx has been exaggerated by its opponents, it is certainly true that Marx features prominently amongst its dialogue partners (just as, liberation theologians are fond of noting, the non-Christian Aristotle provided a point of dialogue for medieval scholasticism). With a few exceptions – notably José Miranda (1974) – liberation theology has selectively borrowed insights from Marx (and subsequent Marxism) in order to acquire tools for understanding the world. The point is made well by Gustavo Gutiérrez (1996):

> In the contemporary intellectual world, including the world of theology, references are often made to Marx and to certain Marxists, and their contribution to the field of social and economic analysis are often taken into account. But these facts do not, in themselves, mean an acceptance of Marxism, especially insofar as Marxism embodies an all-embracing view of life and thus excludes Christian faith and its requirements. (p. 46)

The form of borrowing from Marx envisaged here, then, is minimal. Nevertheless, to the extent that it is representative of liberation theology, it stands under censure from the (Catholic) Congregation for the Doctrine of the Faith, who in their 1984 *Instruction on Certain Aspects of the 'Theology of Liberation'*[7] turned critical attention on liberation theology. At the heart of the concern of the *Instruction*'s authors lies the worry that Marxian social theory cannot be disentangled from Marx's atheism and wider philosophy. Thus,

> Let us recall the fact that atheism and the denial of the human person, his liberty and rights, are at the core of the Marxist theory. This theory, then, contains errors which directly threaten the truths of the faith regarding the eternal destiny of individual persons. Moreover, to attempt to integrate into theology an analysis whose criterion of interpretation depends on this atheistic conception is to involve oneself in terrible contradictions.

Whilst one common response on the part of liberation theologians has been to deny the connection between their favoured social theory and Marxian atheism,

---

[7] www.vatican.va/roman_curia/congregations/cfaith/documents/rc_con_cfaith_doc_19840806_theology-liberation_en.html.

other left-wing theologians have agreed with the *Instruction*, against liberation theology, that Marx's atheism is not easily separable from his social theory; but, rather than seeing this as reason to reject Marx's thought, they have viewed it as pointing to novel opportunities for theological engagement. Prominent in this respect is Alistair Kee's (1990) *Marx and the Failure of Liberation Theology.* Here Kee argues that Marx has an ontological critique of religion, a critique of its belief in God, and that this has been ignored by Christians who make use of Marx – in particular by liberation theologians. Radical Christians, rather than continuing this ignoring, ought to take Marx's ontological critique on board and embrace a substantial doctrine of divine transcendence.

Views similar to Kee's can be identified in authors involved in, or influenced by, the Catholic leftist journal *Slant*, which ran from 1966 to 1970. Associated with authors such as Terry Eagleton, and with Herbert McCabe, who acted as a mentor figure for the group behind *Slant,* the journal pursued a politically left-wing Catholicism influenced by the secular New Left of the period, Wittgenstein, and, crucially for our purposes, Marx (Corrin 2013). The *Slant* authors engaged across the range of Marx's thought, differing from the liberation theologians in their preparedness to think about the existence of God, say, or morality in a way that took Marxist insights on board. In this they anticipated the position of someone like Kee.

This openness to Marx's philosophy is perhaps best seen subsequent to *Slant* in McCabe's taking on board of Marx's atheism and expositing alongside it his own doctrine of God as transcendent and not in competition with creaturely agents (Hewitt 2024). Similarly Eagleton, as Britain's foremost Marxist cultural critic fully cognisant of Marx on religion, repeatedly gestures in a McCabian direction towards a classical theism which coheres with Marx's critique of belief in God (Eagleton 2006; 2010). In like manner Denys Turner (1987), moving in the same milieu, takes Marx's approach to God to transcend the theism–atheism dialectic in a manner consistent with an apophatic doctrine of God.

My approach in this Element is firmly on the side of those theologians who do not ignore Marx's philosophical writing. Not only do I hold that this writing is indispensable to the Marxian corpus but I think that in particular Marx's criticism of religion, read with reference to afterlife belief, poses an urgent challenge to Christian thought and practice which simply cannot be ignored if we are to do that justice to the exploited and oppressed which is required of followers of Christ. What follows is an attempt to explicate, listen to, and take on board that challenge.

Before moving on with that business, mention should be made of the engagement of a prominent theologian with Marx's work, Nicholas Lash's *A Matter of*

Hope (1981). Lash sits within an older tradition of theological reading of Marx than the two described earlier, namely that of dialogue. For the Christian side of this tradition Marx is to be read alongside, compared to, and perhaps criticised in the light of, Christian texts and doctrine. Lash undertakes this task comprehensively and, for someone as sympathetic to Marx as me, challengingly. In particular, Lash believes that Marxism possesses a rival eschatology to Christianity. To that matter we will return.

1.3 On Hell

To conclude this introduction, something should be said about an uncomfortable topic. I have already written about heaven and will later write about the Kingdom of God. What, though, about another traditional topic of Christian eschatology: hell? These days, a theologian who writes about the last things without mentioning hell might be suspected of being a universalist. And universalism is certainly in the theological air at the moment. As a politically engaged theologian, however, I find universalism to be too easy a response to a reality beset with evils. How does one speak of universal salvation faced with genocides, with the imposed suffering of the poor, and with culpable environmental destruction? If there is to be universal salvation in the face of these realities, a universal salvation understood in a manner which is not simply a careless setting aside of horrendous evils, it must be hard won and brought about through a mercy which does not merely ignore or forget but confronts and conquers human evil. We cannot understand such a mercy, and certainly cannot *know* that it will be operative at the end of all things.[8] What we can do is *hope*; and following von Balthasar (1988), I think that this is the right comportment towards the possibility of universal salvation.

If my motivation for not writing about hell (other than here) is not universalism, what is it? It is quite simply that hell is not the subject matter of Christian eschatology in the same sense as heaven, and especially the Kingdom. We are not faced with two equally matched realities, with two possible outcomes for creation. There is an echo here of Rahner's (1978) point regarding individual destiny; heaven and hell are not finely balanced alternatives (p. 435). The creation is destined to be the Kingdom of God, which has been secured definitively in Christ. Hell is, for Christian theology, first and foremost that from which we are saved.[9]

---

[8] As will become clear in Section 5, however, I do think there is a sense in which we can know that God's eschatological vindication of God's people, of the poor and oppressed, will take place.

[9] Which is not to say that belief in hell cannot function in an ideological manner. Think, say, of a woman scared into compliance with patriarchal norms by belief in hell, and by belief that those who do not follow those norms are in danger of hell. It is just that my concern here is with the 'positive' side of Christian eschatology for theological reasons I give in the body of the text.

There is a political aspect to this. The evils I have catalogued earlier, and countless other injustices, do not have the last word in history. That much is a matter of Christian faith. Far from providing a demotivation for political action, this provides us with the hope we need to struggle on in dark times. The powers of hell will be vanquished, and in an important sense have already been vanquished. The final victory is ours, in Christ; it remains for us to fight towards that victory (something can of course be entirely God's action whilst being the result of our agency; God and creatures do not compete for agency (McCabe 1987; Tanner 2004)).

Our faithfulness to that fight will be impeded, however, if we cling to ideas or propagate pictures which reconcile people to an inadequate world. In what follows we will consider how not to do that, learning some lessons from Marx.

2 Marx, the Kingdom, and the Resurrection

Marx's most famous treatment of religion deserves quoting in full:

> The foundation of irreligious criticism is: *Man* [*sic*] *makes religion*, religion does not make man. Religion is, indeed, the self-consciousness and self-esteem of man who has either not yet won through to himself, or has already lost himself again. But *man* is no abstract being squatting outside the world. Man is *the world of man* – state, society. This state and this society produce religion, which is an *inverted consciousness of the world*, because they are an *inverted world*. Religion is the general theory of this world, its encyclopaedic compendium, its logic in popular form, its spiritual *point d'honneur*, its enthusiasm, its moral sanction, its solemn complement, and its universal basis of consolation and justification. It is the *fantastic realization* of the human essence since the *human essence* has not acquired any true reality. The struggle against religion is, therefore, indirectly the struggle *against that world* whose spiritual *aroma* is religion. (Marx [1844] 1970; italics in the original)

Marx continues:

> *Religious* suffering is, at one and the same time, the *expression* of real suffering and a *protest* against real suffering. Religion is the sigh of the oppressed creature, the heart of a heartless world, and the soul of soulless conditions. It is the *opium* of the people.
>
> The abolition of religion as the *illusory* happiness of the people is the demand for their *real* happiness. To call on them to give up their illusions about their condition is to call on them to *give up a condition that requires illusions*. The criticism of religion is, therefore, *in embryo, the criticism of that vale of tears* of which religion is the *halo*.

He reiterates the point using striking imagery:

> Criticism has plucked the imaginary flowers on the chain not in order that man shall continue to bear that chain without fantasy or consolation, but so

that he shall throw off the chain and pluck the living flower. The criticism of religion disillusions man, so that he will think, act, and fashion his reality like a man who has discarded his illusions and regained his senses, so that he will move around himself as his own true Sun. Religion is only the illusory Sun which revolves around man as long as he does not revolve around himself.

Note that here Marx is concerned with religion in its generality, not narrowly with God or the idea of God. The concept of God no doubt falls within the remit of his criticism, but it is the whole panoply of religious belief and practice which is being diagnosed as at once an expression of and an illusory consolation to domination within human society and its effects. In particular belief in, and orientation of life towards, *heaven* seems particularly fertile matter for Marx's critique. Doesn't the belief that all will be well after death seem to be exactly a case of 'the sigh of the oppressed creature, the heart of a heartless world . . . the opium of the people'? Isn't it an illusion which ought to be done away with, an excision from belief and practice which, for Marx, involves '[giving] up [the] condition that requires illusions'?

It is not to the point here for the Christian theologian to insist that belief in heaven is *true*, and therefore that it cannot be illusory. As I will make clear in due course, I share the belief in (something describable as) heaven. In one sense the theologian asserting the reality of heaven is arguing on the same plane as Marx. After all, it should not, indeed cannot, be denied for one moment that Marx thinks that belief in heaven is false. But what is going on in this passage is not simply a stand-off between the theologian and her critic about the truth-value of some propositions concerning the afterlife. Rather, Marx is, as much as anything, concerned with the *function* of eschatological belief. That belief, he claims, both expresses the suffering of oppressed and exploited people (on this much the theologian can surely agree readily) and functions to reconcile them to that suffering. Because it does this, it should be abandoned, and attention directed towards superseding the social conditions that give rise to the hope for heaven. 'Criticism has plucked the imaginary flowers on the chain not in order that man shall continue to bear that chain without fantasy or consolation, but so that he shall throw off the chain and pluck the living flower.'

What about this suggestion concerning eschatological belief, that it has a reconciliatory function? Can the theologian agree with this? On the face of it, she cannot. After all, isn't eschatological belief central to Christianity: confessed in creeds, proclaimed in liturgical celebrations, and thoroughly scriptural? And wouldn't it therefore undermine Christian belief and practice if it were admitted that our beliefs concerning the ultimate destiny of God's people served to make peace with exploitative and oppressive social conditions in a fashion that undermined attempts to transform those conditions?

On the contrary, it is clear that belief in heaven does sometimes, perhaps often, fulfil the function Marx describes. The theologian is not in a position to deny this. The question is what she is to do about it. Here I want to suggest two things: first that the theologian has a prophetic function within the People of God, and that this includes the criticism of the way afterlife belief functions; second, that it is wrong to think of heaven, understood as a spiritual state of souls, as the focus of Christian eschatology. Instead it is the *Kingdom of God* and the *resurrection of the body* which ought to be our primary concern. Recognising these two things will go some way, I think, towards dealing with the reconciliatory function of eschatology. We cannot, however, be glib about this. The function of religion as 'the opium of the people'[10] goes deep and has a habit of returning, even when we think we have undermined that function in favour of a healthier role.

2.1 Prophecy

The figure of the prophet is an important one in the Old Testament,[11] and carries over to (at least) the synoptic gospels in the persons of Jesus and John the Baptist.[12] The role of a prophet is to speak God's word to God's people, and that word is often one of challenge and of condemnation for having failed to observe the covenant. The prophet is not simply an external tribune for the wrongdoings of God's people. Rather the prophet is called out of the People of God in order to speak to, sometimes to criticise, the People of God. Consider, for instance, this passage attributed to the prophet Amos,

> Hear this, you that trample on the needy, and bring to ruin the poor of the land, saying, 'When will the new moon be over so that we may sell grain; and the sabbath, so that we may offer wheat for the sale? We will make the ephah small and the shekel great, and practise deceit with false balances, buying the poor for silver and the needy for a pair of sandals, and selling the sweepings of the wheat.'
>
> The LORD has sworn by the pride of Jacob; Surely I will never forget any of their deeds. Shall not the land tremble on this account, and everyone mourn who lives in it, and all of it rise like the Nile, and be tossed about and sink again, like the Nile of Egypt.[13]

---

[10] It is frequently pointed out that Marx's language of religion as 'the opium of the people' is ambiguous. Opioids relieve pain as well as being the potential cause of damaging addiction. This is true enough, but somehow misses the point that, in context, Marx intends the metaphor to foreground the reconciliatory function of religion.

[11] I prefer this usage to 'Hebrew Bible', first because I accept as canonical books contained in the Septuagint but not in the Hebrew Bible, but more relevantly because it acknowledges that I am reading the text as a Christian, and am not entitled to read it as though I were a Jew.

[12] The theme of prophecy is particularly present in Luke's gospel, where it is developed with respect to the prophet Elijah. See e.g. Kloppenborg and Verheyden 2014.

[13] Amos 9:4–8. NRSV formatting removed.

Of interest here is the way the prophetic author runs together concerns we would call *political* (bringing the poor to 'ruin') with ones we would term *religious* (failures of sabbath observance). Of course we should not in fact make the religion–politics distinction as we read this text. First, there is a good argument to the effect that sabbath observance, along with much of the Torah, is concerned with human well-being, in this case giving servants and others temporary freedom from work, and allowing them to rest. Second, and relatedly, the religion–politics distinction trades on the modern divide between the secular and the sacred, which it is anachronistic to ascribe to voices from ancient Israel.

In spite of the infelicity of terming prophets 'political', we can recognise in their proclamation God's concern for those areas of reality we would now term political. Through the prophets (and Amos is only one example here) God's preferential option for the poor is revealed, and those who exploit the poor are condemned. This condemnation falls frequently against religious practice which ignores the poor. Thus Isaiah,

> Your new moons and your appointed festivals my soul hates; they have become a burden to me, I am weary of bearing them. When you stretch out your hands, I will hide my eyes from you; even though you make many prayers, I will not listen; your hands are full of blood. Wash yourselves; make yourselves clean; remove the evil of your doings from before my eyes; cease to do evil, learn to do good; seek justice, rescue the oppressed, defend the orphan, plead for the widow.[14]

God's call, made through the prophet, is to do justice by the poor. In the absence of such justice, religion is not acceptable to God. In the light of Marx we might add, religion can actively serve to sustain the lot of the poor, reconciling them (and their exploiters) to their condition, not least with tales of a heaven which will follow after, and provide recompense for, their present suffering.

There is then a critique of religion to be made; it is a prophetic critique (albeit one towards which engagement with Marx, and other figures outside religious traditions,[15] can contribute). It is also a critique to which, within a Christian context, all the baptised are called to participate in. Recall here the traditional idea of the threefold office of Christ transmitted to the Church: we are priests, prophets, and rulers.[16]

---

[14] Isaiah 1: 14–17.

[15] I hereby reject the claim sometimes made that Marx *really* stands within the Jewish prophetic tradition, a view which is patronising towards him in not taking his rejection of religion seriously, and subtly antisemitic in its projection of a prophetic mystique onto a Jewish figure who would certainly disown it.

[16] 'Rulers' is usually rendered 'kings'. I have changed this for obvious reasons. The notion of any ruler might be thought, and not without reason, to be politically problematic. I take the rule of

If the calling to prophesy belongs to all the baptised, however, it might very well be argued that there is a particular responsibility on theologians to be prophetic. After all, the theologian articulates critically Christian doctrine (Williams 2000, pp. xii–xv), and as part of this task reflects on Christian practice. Prophecy surely falls within this remit. Further than that, if the theologian is not thinking and writing prophetically, if she is silent in the face of the use of Christian thought and practice to sustain injustice, then she is both complicit in that injustice and failing in her task.

Next in this section I am going to sketch what I think a prophetic theological eschatology might look like, first identifying problems with a common picture of heaven, and then attempting to correct them in the light of another, scriptural, eschatology. Reflecting Marx's concerns, my focus will be on political problems with some eschatologies (and practices based on those eschatologies), and possible ways of transcending these.[17]

2.2 The Problems of Heaven

Here is a picture of the afterlife common amongst Christians. The point of life is to get my soul into heaven. In order to do this my soul must be saved, through the work of Jesus Christ, and perhaps in an associated way with my performance of good works. My soul is immaterial, and separable from my body. Heaven is likewise an immaterial state and (we hope) our ultimate destiny. Christian practice ought to focus on getting to heaven, for example by praying for this.

This picture goes deep, even amongst those who would officially disown it. It is attractive in some ways, as we will see. And whilst I am critical of it in many respects, I do not want to claim that it is entirely false. More than that, I want to claim that it is, in one important respect, true.[18] Indeed the fact that it is not entirely false, and is moreover supported in some aspects by scripture and tradition, makes it all the more dangerous. The picture has a hold on us, and we cannot easily let go of it without feeling that we are abandoning some important component of Christian faith.

The picture is first of all dualistic. It holds that soul and body are separable, and that our ultimate destiny concerns our soul exclusively. Now dualism is common in Christian discourse, popular and academic. It is against this background that feminist liberation theologians Ivone Gebara and Maria Clara

---

Christ (and of his People) to be ironic, subverting the norms of oppressive rule, not least through being shared. More needs to be said about this.

[17] The project of resourcing political alternatives from scripture and Christian tradition has been criticised in Rose 2023. Engaging with that criticism is business for elsewhere.

[18] See next section.

Bingemer (1989) write about an 'idealist anthropology' which is intimately involved with dualism. (p. 7) They tell us,

> Idealism, like dualism to which it is closely linked, is always tempting to us. The world of our dreams and projections is always beautiful, harmonious, perfect. The real world in which we live, with its constant conflicts, its apparent or real contradictions, seems to weigh us down. Our desire changes the world; very often we live wrapped up in the world we desire or project, and we forget to look at its beauty and ugliness, its cleanliness or filth. What most interests us is the 'other world,' the 'other me,' the 'other reality.'

In a related vein, in his *Theology after Wittgenstein*, much of which is a sustained invocation of that philosopher against dualist theological anthropology, Fergus Kerr (1997, p. 168) writes of,

> The mentalist-individualist conception of the self [which] owes much of its imaginative power and psychological appeal to the vitality of the myth of the soul as a ghost inside the body. In more specifically Christian terms, it is the Origenist theology which secretes a philosophy of psychology that tends to represent human beings as angels fallen into flesh.

What is it about dualism which makes it a target for a prophetic theology informed by Marx? How, for example, does it effect reconciliation between the victims of oppression and exploitation and their condition? How is it one of the 'flowers', imaginary or otherwise, which need to be 'plucked' off the chain in order that human beings might be free? First, let us focus on the account of the human person implicit in dualism. Far from Aquinas's protestation that 'my soul is not me'[19] being taken on board, it is very much the case for a typical dualist that my soul, immaterial and separable from my body, *is* me. What I am, at the most fundamental level, is not a material being, an animal, but (as Descartes had it) a thinking being. And I can in principle go on being a thinking being without my body.[20] Now this account has the potential to reconcile people to exploitation and oppression in the following way. If I am really to be identified with an immaterial soul then whatever corporeal harm is inflicted upon me – whether it be by employers or governments, sexists or racists – there is always a story to be told according to which that harm cannot really touch me, the *real* me. Given this, I might as well resign myself to the harm, not least because in the fullest sense it is not me being harmed, or at least not any part or aspect of me that will persist as long as my soul. A religious flavour can be given to the account by stressing that it

---

[19] Ad Cor. I.15.

[20] So the dualistic picture has it. In reality, our cognitive activity is a thoroughly bodily affair, and not just because of it being tied up with our brains. Think, for example, about the role of those most bodily of states – emotions – in our thinking, or about how intimately linked are cognition and perception.

is my God-given duty to ensure that my soul is saved and to keep it pristine. Again, reconciliation to injustice can readily be effected by this idea.

Before we go on to think about the role of pictures of heaven in a religious worldview that can be criticised on Marxian grounds, it is important to note some other deleterious consequences of dualistic views of the human person. Foremost amongst these is surely the interaction between dualistic accounts of the human person and gender. For once human beings are conceived as consisting of body and a distinct soul (or spirit, or mind), with the former being more important, it is the case distressingly often that women are associated with the body, men with the soul (Lennon 2019). Given that the soul, on the relevant picture, is more important than the body, a justification for patriarchy ensues, whether assented to consciously or unconsciously. Similar associations with body and soul can surely be recognised in relation to race and sexuality. Moreover, dualistic views tend to downplay the importance of non-human animals, which – it is thought – belong solely to the realm of the bodily. These views also do not bode well for concern about the natural environment; this, after all, is part of a material world to which we do not, according to dualism, ultimately belong.

Back to doing prophetic theology with Marx. What challenge does he present for belief concerning heaven? Suppose that heaven is our destiny, that what really matters is getting to heaven. Suppose further that heaven is disjoint with this material world. Both of these are implicit in the picture of the afterlife set out at the beginning of this subsection. Now, what is Marx going to say about this picture? He would first of all set about explaining the hold the picture has on us, situating its origins in the multiple alienations of our material lives. He would then go on to lay out the ways in which the picture reconciles us to our lot. As well as the ways mentioned previously, implicit in the picture is the view that what really matters for human beings[21] is getting to heaven. Our earthly lives are merely a pilgrimage, a means to this, and ought to be regarded as unimportant in the light of our heavenly destiny.[22] It is straightforward to see how this can reconcile people to earthly suffering, exploitation and oppression. If my work is hard and unrewarding I have, at best, a highly reduced incentive to fight this – through trade union activity, say – if my working life is only a precursor to my

---

[21] In passing, the question of the eschatological destiny of non-human beings, too often dismissed as issuing from mere sentimentality, deserves a lot more treatment than it customarily gets.

[22] This view has a hold not only at the level of popular piety. Consider many philosophical treatments of the problem of evil, for which a future afterlife justifies present sufferings (cf. Kilby 2020, ch. 6). The view described in the final subsection of this section is importantly different from this, since there is no sense there that the Kingdom justifies the sufferings of the millions of human beings who have lived in the run-up to it, but rather that those people share in the victory over those sufferings. Pain and death are not *justified*, they are defeated.

being in heaven. 'You'll get pie in the sky when you die.' Recall further that according to the picture we are considering, heaven is discontinuous with my earthly life. It is not the case that improving my working life has in any sense a bearing on the nature of my eschatological destiny. So I might well cultivate a disinterested attitude towards my earthly existence, or at least feel that I should. The only things in my earthly life that really matter are my sins and my merits, since these (at least on some views) have a bearing on my eternal destiny. This life is a means to an end, namely getting into heaven, and is not the occasion to fight for a better world (unless, of course, I see this fight as a means of acquiring merit, but even then the fight is fundamentally instrumental and not integral to eschatology).

There are, of course, plenty of scriptural passages which can be read in support of the view of the afterlife being criticised here. 'Store up for yourselves treasures in heaven'[23]; 'Do not fear those who kill the body but cannot kill the soul'.[24] It is, however, worth recognising the extent to which readings of these as supportive of this view may be the result of a theological picture having a hold on us, and therefore being open to the possibility that exposure to an alternative picture might bring us to a situation where we can read the passages differently.

Now, the point of this engagement with Marx is not to dismiss belief in an afterlife for political reasons, nor even to dispense entirely with the concept of heaven. This concept will be a concern of the next section. Instead, what I propose is taking a Marxist attitude towards a disembodied afterlife, disjoint with this world, on board and using it to motivate theology in a prophetic mode, exploring scriptural alternatives to dualistic and reconciliatory understandings of the afterlife. Doing this is the business of the next section.

2.3 Kingdom and Resurrection

Do scripture and Christian tradition provide us with an alternative to the reconciliatory eschatology described earlier? The point in asking this question is not to provide an easy means of dismissing the Marxian critique; that critique goes deep. Rather, my purpose is to sketch out a better eschatology than the one we have just dealt with, and to do so with an eye to the Marxian criticisms.

Recall that the picture we had cause to criticise in Secion 2.2 is fundamentally dualistic; the material world, and in particular our bodies, is a means to an end. That end is life in heaven. Attempts to improve the world, to the extent that they matter at all, are understood in instrumental terms. At best they are a means of getting to heaven. I am now going to suggest the basics of an eschatology which

---

[23] Matthew 6:20; cf. Luke 12:33.   [24] Matthew 10:28; cf. Luke 2:4–5.

avoids these features, one centred on the resurrection of the body and the Kingdom of God.

Take the resurrection of the body first. In spite of its de-emphasis in much contemporary Christianity, this doctrine is both scriptural and credal: 'I believe in ... the resurrection of the body' proclaims the ancient baptismal formulary known as the Apostles' Creed. Now there are good reasons that belief in the resurrection of the body has gone out of favour. How can we hold the doctrine, it might be asked, when we know that bodies rot, are blown up in wars, are cremated, and so on? From what, naively but to the point, runs the question, does God resurrect my body? Some answer here can be had by reflecting on Paul's words,

> There are heavenly bodies and there are earthly bodies, but the glory of the heavenly is of one kind, and the glory of the earthly is of another. There is one glory of the sun, and another glory of the moon, and another glory of the stars; indeed, star differs from star in glory ... It is sown a physical[25] body; it is raised a spiritual body.[26]

It is, for Paul, our physical body which is buried and rots (or, we might add with an eye to contemporary circumstances, is cremated). We are destined to have spiritual bodies. These may not pose the same difficulties around resurrection as physical bodies. Much more could be said about this in a work of greater length (in particular, the issue should be addressed of whether the physical body and the spiritual body are numerically identical). The crucial point for us, however, is that there is scriptural witness to the human destiny being bodily.

This goes some way towards answering the charge of dualism (although some work needs to be done on the contrast between natural/physical and spiritual: it is easy to read into this a renewed dualism).[27] What it does not do, of itself, is answer the charge of reconciliation to exploitation and oppression. I may believe that my ultimate future is bodily, but still regard my bodily life here and now as merely a stepping stone *en route* to the resurrection, and so not be concerned with improving current life.

It is at the point that the idea of the Kingdom of God becomes salient. The Kingdom of God, preached by Jesus, is an all-encompassing reality. We cannot separate off a 'political' part of the Kingdom or an aspect to do with post-mortem destiny. Instead, the Kingdom, which is already seen here and now when people love or struggle for justice, will come to completion by God's gift

---

[25] English Standard Version 'natural'. Gk. *psuchikon*.   [26] 1 Corinthians 15:40–1; 44.

[27] Interestingly Aquinas parses this kind of language in Paul in a non-dualistic way, seeing it as marking a distinction between someone spiritually dead and someone spiritually alive (Turner 2022, p. 7).

when the whole of creation is renewed. The Kingdom has been inaugurated, and our efforts on its behalf contribute to it, but it is also *not yet*, we await the final fulfilment of the Kingdom. These themes have been developed, of course, by liberation theologians, but also, in English, by the tradition associated with Kenneth Leech (2001, pp. 220–2), which is often undervalued by academic theologians.

Because the Kingdom is all-encompassing, so both politically inflected[28] and body-involving (and therefore tied up with the resurrection of the dead), it provides us with a basis on which to construct an eschatology which is sensitive to Marx's critique. Because there is continuity with our life here and now, and because our struggles are part of the building up of the Kingdom,[29] it looks as though an eschatology which is Kingdom-focused need not be either dualistic or reconciliatory.

Yet this might seem a little bit too neat. It could give the impression of having answered Marx's critique. But that critique could be repeated in the following way. The Kingdom in its fulness is in the future. But our struggle against exploitation and oppression is in the here and now. In focusing on a future where everything is healed, Christian eschatology is guilty of utopianism. In fact, this response insists, this future eschatology provides an imaginary recon-ciliation of a real contradiction just as surely does a heaven focused eschatology.

Faced with this renewed critique, proponents of a Kingdom-based eschat-ology can only commit themselves to living with the tension between *now* and *not-yet*. Their challenge is to engage in present struggles, looking to the future fulness of the Kingdom as a source of hope, without allowing that future-orientated hope to demotivate their struggles or reconcile them to present injustice. In living out this tension, Marx's critique is a valuable corrective.

3 After Death and before the Kingdom

To summarise some of the previous section, the Christian hope is to be resur-rected into the fullness of the Kingdom,[30] a Kingdom which is continuous with our present struggles. This could, albeit in a fashion that requires living with ongoing tension, appear to provide us with an eschatology which does not

---

[28] Or, more carefully, politically inflected from a present perspective. The Kingdom represents the end of politics when it comes in its fullness; there will be no more need for struggles for justice. Here and now, however, work for the Kingdom cannot but be political.

[29] Which is not to say that the Kingdom at every moment is not divine gift. Divine and human agency do not compete: we build the Kingdom, God gives the Kingdom. Both are true.

[30] Some authors hold that resurrection is immediate, and does not wait until the Kingdom comes in its fullness. See van Dyke 2012, and for discussion of this topic Yates 2017. My own view is that this position is individualistic and doesn't sufficiently capture the corporate and Kingdom-centred nature of Christian hope in the face of death. See Hewitt 2022.

collapse in the face of Marx's critique. What is absent from that eschatology as I've just stated it is any mention of an intermediate state. That is, I have said nothing about the period between death and resurrection. Traditionally Christians have held that the 'soul' of a person survives death and exists between death and the resurrection. Some Christians engage in practices related to this belief: prayer for the dead, for example, and seeking the prayers of the saints. But this belief in an intermediate state looks far more prone to Marx's critique than belief in the resurrection.

Why is that? First, because we naturally conceive of an intermediate state in dualistic terms, hearing the word 'soul' as synonymous with Cartesian 'mind'.[31] Second, because it seems to downplay the importance of death: the dead no longer seem really dead, and this in turn makes us sit lightly to death. 'The heart of a heartless world' here justifies both war and capital punishment. Third, because belief in an intermediate state detracts from the final coming of the Kingdom in its fullness, and therefore from work towards that Kingdom.

On the contrary, I think that it is possible to recover a version of belief in an intermediate state which need not vanish in the wake of Marxist criticism. This version has to continue to be sobered by engagement with Marx, and in particular to somehow relate the immediate post-mortem destiny of whatever we mean by 'the soul' to ongoing political struggle. To that end, I will lay out an account of the soul which is more deflated than those implicit in much current Christianity, and which is non-dualistic. In the course of this, I will say something to the first and third objections given earlier. Before articulating my account, however, something should be said to the second objection.

3.1 The Dead Really Are Dead

Are the dead not really dead? Marxist theorist Mark Neocleous has linked an affirmative answer to this question to fascism.[32] Alarming though the drawing of this connection may be, it is important for the politically engaged theologian to be aware of it, and to understand how politically charged the dead, especially in the case of fascism the *war* dead, can be. For fascism, the dead, containing in themselves the past of the nation in the present, fight alongside the nation's armies. Hitler at one point declaimed, 'Long live our Volk! And may today the dead of our Movement, Germany and its men, living and dead, live on!'[33] In passing it is important to note that Neocleous also identifies the trope of resurrection amongst fascist movements who deny that the dead are really

---

[31] For this reason Herbert McCabe (2000) produced a catechism which didn't once speak of the soul. I will not quite follow him in this here, but it is completely understandable. We are prone to get trapped in a Cartesian way of viewing the world.
[32] Neocleous 2005, ch. 3.   [33] Neocleous 2005, p. 105.

dead. It is vital therefore that the Christian who wants to proclaim the doctrine of resurrection, as described in the previous section, links it to the Kingdom of justice, love and peace, a Kingdom which – by contrast with fascist 'resurrection' – is not national. The idea of the resurrection of the dead, rather than being a promise of new life, can become something monstrous, a long way from affirming life.

Whilst not fascist, there are other political and social practices which are backed up by belief that the dead are not really dead, that their soul persists in heaven, and is to be identified with them. This belief functions *ideologically* in Marx's sense.[34] As observed in the previous subsection both war and capital punishment, and we might add sitting lightly to climate change, can be supported this way. If death does not, at the most fundamental level end the life of the dead,[35] then there is a disincentive to worry too much about state-sanctioned killing, whether on the lethal injection gurney or in the battlefield. If, moreover, our home is ultimately in some spiritual situation disjoint from this physical universe, the threat of our planet becoming uninhabitable fades into the background. Minimising death, which is what the claim that the dead are not really dead does, is politically dangerous.

It is worth observing that the consequences of this minimisation are not simply political, at least in a straightforward sense of that word. Although our main interlocutor here is Marx, it is useful to turn briefly to another of the 'masters of suspicion',[36] Freud.

In his much-maligned work on mourning,[37] Freud (1917) maintains that a healthy, conscious, processing of loss on the part of the bereaved person involves what Freud calls grief-work, culminating in detachment from the object of their loss. Failure to detach is pathological. This has been met with no small amount of objections: that it is an unfeeling approach to grief and that it ignores the important and ongoing role deceased people can play in the lives of the bereaved. Now, especially in a theological context, I do not want to deny the possibility of such a role; we will meet later on a way of thinking about an intermediate state which makes sense of prayer for the departed, and

---

[34] Ideology, for Marx, is a collection of beliefs and/or practices, produced within some social order and distorting it, which functions to shore up that social order (Marx and Engels 1845). There has been a considerable amount of debate within Marxism on the precise boundaries and contours of ideology.

[35] In passing, I can only read the Catholic eucharistic preface for masses for the dead which declares 'life is changed not ended' as a tacit rejection of the view that there is no intermediate state. If it is not doing that, it is false.

[36] The term is Ricœur's (1970, p. 33).

[37] For example, theorists and practitioners around the approach to grief known as Continuing Bonds (Klass and Steffen 2018) have been highly critical of Freud. On my reading of the Freudian tradition here, there is more room for rapprochement than is usually thought.

memorialisation of the dead in various ways is integral to religious practice. But one way of developing the Freudian thought is not that no mention should be made of the dead; rather it is that it is important to come to the recognition that *the dead are dead*, that we can no longer continue with them as we did before, and that our lives must develop in a way that is, in an important sense, without the dead. These recognitions are important for healthy functioning, since without them we will be insensitive to reality and closed off to possibilities. To put it in Christian terms, which are certainly not Freud's, the undetached person will be impervious to potential calls from God to live in new ways that do not directly involve the lost person.

With Freud and against those who would claim otherwise, it is important to insist that the dead really are dead, that their life has ceased, and a great harm has been done to them. Indeed it seems oxymoronic to say that someone *survives death*; anyone making this profession surely doesn't understand what the verb 'to survive' means. More concretely, we are bodily creatures, our life is that of animals, living in a material world created by God, and flourishing, in so much as we do, precisely as the kind of things we are. If our animal life is annihilated, we are annihilated. If we are to live again, it can only be through the restoration of bodily life in the final resurrection. We do not *have* bodies, after all, we *are* bodies, living bodies. And all of this being the case, the dead really are dead.

3.2 A Non-dualistic Soul

Is there any way, in the light of this facing up to the reality of death, of maintaining belief in an intermediate state? The answer might seem to be a resounding 'no'. And this is a natural answer from those who have excised from themselves a dualistic view of the human person, through engagement with Marx or otherwise. Yet there is a long tradition, normative for many Christians, of believing that 'the soul' persists after death and, as I have noted, there are liturgical and devotional practices tied up with this belief. Can we make sense of these?[38]

We cannot make sense of them if we understand the soul dualistically, as a *thing* which is for a time united to a human body, but only accidentally, and able to flourish (even perhaps flourish more, *freed* from the body) without a body. In contrast with this dualism, pre-Cartesian authors, especially Aquinas, emphasised the idea that the soul is the *form of the body*. We might parse this in terms of an organism's particular way of being alive. And human beings are a particular kind of organism, namely rational animals.[39] We engage in what Marx (1845) called 'practical critical activity'. Moreover we are

---

[38] I have presented what follows in greater detail in Hewitt 2022.

[39] There is no need to claim that human beings are unique in this.

equipped with language[40] and can make conceptual sense of the world, as well as telling stories about ourselves: we are narrative creatures.[41] Now if we identify the soul with a rational animal's being alive in this particular kind of way, we can perhaps identify the intermediate state with the persistence of a person's narrative in the eyes of God:[42] the narrative may need healing (thus purgatory; we might talk here of editing), can be remembered before God (thus seeking the intercession of the saints), and may be held in the light of God's glory (thus beatitude). It is secure, rather than being dependent on mortal memory or memorialisation, and will once again be the story of a living person at the resurrection of the dead. In the meanwhile, there is not a living person of whom it is the story, because its subject is dead.

3.3 All in the Light of the Kingdom

So perhaps we can preserve a deflationary account of an intermediate state. This cannot, however, be allowed to displace the Kingdom as the focus of Christian eschatology. Partly this is because of the kind of ethico-political considerations we have met through engagement with Marx; our struggles are directed towards the Kingdom, and find their fulfilment in it. It is also because of the primacy of the theme of the Kingdom of God in the gospels, and because justice can only be done to the goodness and giftedness of the corporeal creation and the social nature of our lives if these things are preserved eschatologically.

The key theological task, then, is to show how an account of an intermediate state need not crowd out the Kingdom as an eschatological theme. A starting point here is to note that what is preserved post-mortem in the previous account are narratives, not persons.[43] The dead really are dead. There is a real rupture involved in death, and if we want to talk about persons living again after their death, appeal to the intermediate state will not suffice. We need to invoke more all-encompassing eschatological concepts, and these are the Kingdom and the resurrection of the body.

Merely noting this, however, does not explain the connections between the intermediate state and the Kingdom in other than a sequential fashion: *first* there is the intermediate state, and *then* the Kingdom comes in all its fullness. Is there no deeper connection between them other than this purely extrinsic one? The

---

[40] Jones 2018, citing Marx and Engels 1845.

[41] This has been denied by Galen Strawson 2004. I do not know how to argue against his position. It seems to me that someone who takes that position needs to be *shown* the importance of narrative to human life, not argued into believing in it.

[42] I've written elsewhere about the narrative being preserved 'from the inside'. This needs a lot more fleshing out but is work for another occasion.

[43] I'm using 'persons' rather than 'people' here in accordance with philosophical custom.

beginnings of thought about such a connection can be had by noting that the life narratives of human persons are intrinsically political. Our stories are affected by the social and political circumstances under which we live and we, to differing extents, are socio-political agents, transforming, or abstaining from transforming those circumstances.[44] Now all of these things have a bearing on the Kingdom, as it is understood here: we are harmed because the Kingdom is not yet fully realised; we flourish because the Kingdom has already come in some respect; we struggle for the Kingdom; we fail to struggle for the Kingdom, or even actively struggle against it. The narratives of those of us who suffer or do all of these things can be thought of and taken up in the intermediate state, preserved as part of our story when they belong to the Kingdom, healed when they do not, reconciled with the stories of others alongside whom we suffer and struggle. When the Kingdom comes in its fullness, these healed narratives will once again become our stories, as we inhabit a reality in which Kingdom-orientated struggle is fulfilled and it is finally apparent how our disparate stories relate to that fulfilment.

The point here is that the Kingdom, whilst entirely a divine gift, is also built up through the lives and work of billions of people. When it is fully realised, the impact of those lives and work will become apparent anew, as the inhabitants of the Kingdom. All this effort is not simply annihilated in the Kingdom, but is part of who people are; it is their narrative, a narrative they will own in fellowship with others and in the vision of God's glory.

3.4 Back to Marx's Critique

Why is this not a subtle renewal of the promise of 'pie in the sky when you die'? Doesn't Marx's critique hit home against belief in an intermediate state'? We have to acknowledge that there is something in this line of questioning. After all, any talk of an intermediate state opens the door to the worry that we are proposing 'the heart of a heartless world'. Because of the conceptual connections which characterise our culture, we are likely to hear talk of 'heaven', even of 'purgatory', in a way such that Marx's critique hits home. If there are these states after death, oughtn't we to focus our attention in living on those, rather than on earthly matters?[45] And what I have offered in Section 3.2 is an account of heaven and of purgatory. So isn't there a problem?

---

[44] I take it that abstaining from transforming ones circumstances is actually, consciously or otherwise, assent to those circumstances. Compare the words often attributed to Desmond Tutu, 'If you are neutral in situations of injustice, you have chosen the side of the oppressor'.

[45] There is, of course, plenty of apparent scriptural warrant for de-emphasising the 'earthly' or 'worldly', for example Matthew 6:19–21; Luke 12:4; Romans 8:9). My strategy here is to say that the problematic readings of these texts issue from our being caught up in a dualist world-view. The earthly, or worldly, ought not to be understood in terms of the here and now material life we live, but rather in terms of that which militates against the coming of the future Kingdom.

It might seem rather inadequate at this point to insist that the account of the intermediate state laid out above does not risk these problems. Dualistic and immediately consolatory conceptions of an afterlife have a grip on us, one that lies deep within our history and society, and even if we have intellectually rejected them, they are likely to continue to surface in our thinking and practice. Theology is not powerless, though, in the face of these hidden ideas. We theologians can lay out views like that sketched in Section 3.2 and by doing so get some purchase on the ideas in question, challenging them and inviting those holding them to a more liberative understanding. And we can, on the basis of the earlier account, insist it is through this current existence that our narratives are formed, narratives which are destined to be ours again in a Kingdom built, not least, out of our political struggles. Those struggles matter because they are Kingdom-building. It is simply a mistake, then, to ignore the here and now in favour of an afterlife. It is the here and now out of which the Kingdom will be formed.

However, the alternatives to this view are not simple or silly prejudices. They arise out of our lives. People seek comfort in an afterlife discontinuous with the here and now because the here and now is so often nightmarish. To approach the matter in a Marxian mode, there is an imperative to fight to supersede the social conditions that lead people to seek imaginary consolation in an afterlife, in a way that reconciles them to current exploitation and oppression. 'To call on them to give up their illusions about their condition is to call on them to *give up a condition that requires illusions.*'[46] Our battle against ways of thinking about the intermediate state that devalue the here and now, its joys and its struggles, cannot be solely an intellectual one. Whilst there is undoubtedly room for intellectual, theological, interventions against the kind of conceptions which pose this threat, we must also – for Marx, primarily – work to overcome the alienations which give birth to these conceptions.

To echo what was said in the previous section: there is no neat conclusion here which enables us to dispatch Marx's critique as definitively answered. Eschatological belief of any sort will, at least under present social conditions, be the object of potential scrutiny in respect of its possible reconciliatory role, and it must subject itself to such scrutiny.[47] What I have attempted to provide in this section is an account of the intermediate state that needn't succumb to Marx's critique. Holding to such an account does not remove tension from our believing and practice, but it does perhaps enable us to believe and practise with integrity in the light of political critiques of Christian faith.

---

[46] Marx 1844.

[47] That is, we need to do *critical theology* in Williams' sense (2000, pp. xii–xv).

4 The Politics of Remembrance

Quoting from scripture, Marx once wrote 'let the dead bury their dead'.[48] In context he was applying the text to revolutionary politics; revolutions cannot be constrained by the past but must be grounded in, and take their content from, the present, with an ear to the future:

> The social revolution of the nineteenth century cannot take its poetry from the past but only from the future. It cannot begin with itself before it has stripped away all superstition about the past. The former revolutions required recollections of past world history in order to smother their own content. The revolution of the nineteenth century must let the dead bury their dead in order to arrive at its own content. There the phrase went beyond the content – here the content goes beyond the phrase.

What in the gospel text is hyperbole, a means of conveying the radical demands of the Kingdom, seems to be taken by Marx here with deadly seriousness: it is the present, and in no way the past, out of which radical change can spring. This cannot but have implications for attitudes towards the dead.

Christians meanwhile proclaim 'I believe in … the communion of saints'. Not only do prayer for and to the souls of the deceased play a part in much Christian practice but, as in secular society, memorialisation of the dead, telling stories about the dead, and so on are commonplace. And, as was argued in the previous section, merely taking on board Freud's warning about the need for detachment doesn't render these practices illegitimate. But doesn't Marx seem to think they are precisely that, illegitimate?

He certainly thinks they are *politically* irrelevant, but there are voices in the Marxist tradition – one voice in particular being that of Walter Benjamin – which demur from this. The purpose of this section is to articulate a politics of remembrance drawing on resources from the Marxist tradition, and then to comment on it theologically, in the light of the ideas that have been developed thus far.

Benjamin famously insisted that revolt was nourished 'on the picture of enslaved forebears, not on the ideal of the emancipated heirs' ([1940] 2005, Thesis XII). There is no sitting lightly to the past, or to the dead, here. But neither is there anything of the fascist sense that the dead are still with us. There is simply an appeal to the enslavement of the now dead and a recognition of its enduring political power. We will engage with Benjamin further in Section 4.2. Before that we should turn to another very different political attitude towards death and the dead.

---

[48] Marx 1852, ch. 1; Luke 9:60; Matthew 8:22.

4.1 Radical Mourning

We began with an exert from Joe Hill's 'The Preacher and the Slave'. Hill was a union organiser who was executed by the state of Utah in 1915 on a fabricated murder charge. In the run-up to his death he wrote words that are now routinely rendered 'Don't mourn, organise!' To this day these words are frequently quoted on the part of left-wing activists when there is a death amongst their numbers or of an admired figure. On the face of it, the imperative is a good one: there is a lot against which we should organise, and doing so might seem to be the best possible memorial for the dead. Weeping at the graveside, it could appear, is senseless, a misdirection of energies which might be better spent improving the world. This line of thought is particularly tempting in cases where the deceased person was a victim of unjust structures – as, of course, was Joe Hill. Through fighting on their behalf against those structures, a task that takes priority over any process of mourning, we somehow make reparation for their victimhood and their death. Something like Marx's critique of religion resurfaces here: the business of mourning, whether religious or secular in form, reconciles us to something to which we ought not to be reconciled, namely the death-dealing society which is the context for our grief, and we should turn our attention from that reconciliatory practice to liberative political action. 'Let the dead bury their dead.'

As with the picture of heaven we had reason to critique in previous sections, there is much that is true and worthwhile in this account. This should be emphasised, because when as boldly stated as it was in the previous paragraph, it can appear cold, lacking in appropriate human concern. It is indeed this, and there will be ample opportunity to criticise it for this reason presently, but what the account does insist on, correctly in my view, is that the experience of another's death can, and should, spur us on to action. This will be a theme as this section develops.

Part of the problem with the comportment towards death summed up by 'don't mourn, organise!' is that it fails to recognise the deceased as a person, as someone whose being injured or lost is deserving of recognition. In refusing to mourn the dead, we are as it were co-operating with whatever harm was done to them during life, setting aside their dignity as a person in life and in death.[49] The intelligibility of this kind of talk of someone having dignity in death needn't turn on belief in an afterlife, although it sits very comfortably with the soul-as-narrative view sketched out earlier. It suffices here to think of many of our non-religious contemporaries, who will readily express concern over 'dishonouring' the dead.

---

[49] Compare here Sophocles' *Antigone*.

As well as failing to recognise properly the person who has died, reluctance to mourn fails to recognise that there has been a genuine loss which stands in need of acknowledgement. Death involves a loss of value from the world. This is the case even in the light of an acceptable Christian eschatology: remember, the dead really *are* dead. It is certainly the case from a purely secular perspective. Something important has been lost when a person dies, and it is necessary to devote time to acknowledge this. If this does not happen there is an ironic sense in which, far from setting the deceased aside in the spirit of 'don't mourn organise', we remain undetached from them, in the Freudian sense, and so are hampered by an unacknowledged grief, unable to incorporate those we have lost into a way of seeing reality on which they have really been lost. In order to organise effectively, therefore, we must first mourn. Might it be that Christian theology and practice provides a context in which mourning can take place?

If failure to mourn is one inadequate politically motivated response to death, more striking is what I will call *death-denial*. Not to be confused with the fascist sense of the dead being with us and fighting with us, this left-wing attitude is again undetached in its not recognising the genuine, radical separation of death. It is somewhat apparent in the commonly used obituary slogan 'rest in power', as though the dead were still comrades in the same sense as before. It is also audible in a well-known song about Joe Hill:

> I dreamed I saw Joe Hill last night
> Alive as you and me
> Says I 'But Joe, you're ten years dead'
> 'I never died' says he
> 'I never died' says he.

Another verse continues the theme:

> 'The Copper Bosses killed you Joe;
> They shot you Joe', says I.
> 'Takes more than guns to kill a man'
> Says Joe 'I didn't die'
> Says Joe 'I didn't die'.

Admittedly the context is set as being a dream, although the song quickly moves away from that being apparent. However, the content of the narrated dream is entirely death denying in the most obvious way possible. The subject did not die at all, and any surprise at his ongoing role is entirely misplaced. In passing, it should be said, in a world in which violence is a relentless reality, the suggestion that it takes 'more than guns' to kill someone is less radical than it might seem. The sniper, the regimental soldier, and the gangster all kill with guns. I am writing this days after Israeli gunmen killed two women, Nahida Khalil Anton and Samar

Kamal Anton, in a Palestinian church.[50] Their victims are truly and – but for the *eschaton* – permanently dead. Denying this risks turning our eyes somewhat away from the horror of their killing. And, to generalise, sitting lightly to death risks refusing to confront it as the reality it is.

There is a political importance to death denial, as there is to the closely related avoidance of the reality of death. Neoliberal capitalist society, concerned as it is with ceaselessly transgressing boundaries, hungry always for more, hides death. After all death is a perpetual reminder of our limitedness, of our fragility and finitude. It is a witness to the fact that we can neither work nor consume for ever. So it is concealed in hospitals and buried under euphemisms. Marxist literary critic Terry Eagleton remarks about contemporary US society,

> American culture is deeply hostile to the idea of limit, and therefore to human biology. Postmodernism is obsessed by the body and terrified of biology. The body is a wildly popular topic in US cultural studies – but this is the plastic, remouldable, socially constructed body, not the piece of matter that sickens and dies. Because death is the absolute failure to which we all eventually come, it has not been the most favoured of topics for discussion in the United States. The US distributors of the British film *Four Weddings and a Funeral* fought hard, if unsuccessfully, to change the title. (Eagleton 2003a, pp. 185–6)

Whilst, of course, there are particular cultural factors at play in different places, the phenomenon Eagleton describes is not confined to the US. Neoliberalism, a particular form of capitalism which encourages those living under it to think of themselves as entrepreneurial agents, has been globally prolific in recent decades and requires of those living under it a strenuous ambition and a perpetual forward-lookingness that is quite antithetical to facing the reality of our fragile mortal nature. Nor is it simply neoliberal societies which impose this kind of restless transgression; capitalism itself perpetually moves beyond limits. Famously Marx and Engels have this to say about capitalist society,

> The bourgeoisie cannot exist without constantly revolutionising the instruments of production, and thereby the relations of production, and with them the whole relations of society. Conservation of the old modes of production in unaltered form, was, on the contrary, the first condition of existence for all earlier industrial classes. Constant revolutionising of production, uninterrupted disturbance of all social conditions, everlasting uncertainty and agitation distinguish the bourgeois epoch from all earlier ones. All fixed, fast-frozen relations, with their train of ancient and venerable prejudices and opinions, are swept away, all new-formed ones become antiquated before they can ossify. All that is solid melts into air, all

---

[50] www.vaticannews.va/en/world/news/2023-12/in-gaza-israelis-attack-holy-family-parish-two-women-killed.html.

that is holy is profaned, and man is at last compelled to face with sober senses his real conditions of life, and his relations with his kind. (Marx and Engels 1848)

As the last sentence reveals, Marx and Engels do not view capitalism's frenetic destructiveness of all that lies in the way of accumulation as straightforwardly bad. It strips away the illusions of feudal society, and with them the idea that unequal social relations are given eternally, decreed by God and not to be overturned. In spite of this, though, there is clearly something untrue to our finite nature about capitalism's relentless bringing about of change. In particular, it is unsurprising that societies founded on this drive to transgress will contain a wariness of engaging with death, the ultimate stasis, the final barrier in the way of otherwise perpetual change and unending novelty. And if we are wary of death, we will also be wary of mourning, which is an uncomfortable witness to death.

The kind of societies we inhabit, then, are ones conducive to a flight from acknowledging our finitude and fragility. There are plenty of theological problems with this, not least that the ideal subject of capitalist society, unconstrained by corporeality, indeed immortal, looks very much like God as classically conceived. There are political problems too. The only kind of politics deserving of assent on the part of human beings is a 'politics of human frailty', to use Christopher Insole's (2004) phrase.[51] Such a politics allows us to flourish as the kind of things – mortal, vulnerable, limited – that we in fact are. Such a politics will rail against societies which avoid death. It will also make space for mourning.

So, it seems as though there is a good case for not avoiding mourning. What does the Christian tradition have to offer here? It may not seem as though there is much to distinguish that tradition from the kind of death-avoidant attitudes we have had reason to critique. Augustine notoriously castigated himself for his mourning of a friend (*Confessions* 4.4.7). Paul writes to the Thessalonians:

> But we do not want you to be uninformed, brothers and sisters, about those who have died, so that you may not grieve as others do who have no hope. For since we believe that Jesus died and rose again, even so, through Jesus, God will bring with him those who have died.[52]

But note, Paul is not saying that the recipients of his letter should not grieve. He is counselling them not to grieve *as those who have no hope*. Their grief is set within the context of eschatological hope, a hope that ultimately God 'will bring with [Jesus] those who have died'. Mourning is set in a context which in no way obviates the need for it, but which situates it in a broader framework. In particular, the Kingdom-focused eschatology favoured in this Element

---

[51] As will be obvious, I reject the political liberalism which Insole supports. However, with him I affirm the need for our politics to be one which sits well with frail human beings.
[52] 1 Thessalonians 4:13–8.

allows us to make connections between our hope for the ultimate redemption of the dead and struggles for a better world. It is in the Kingdom, towards which our struggles are orientated, that the dead will again find life. Yet it remains the case that at this moment there has been a genuine loss, and that the dead really are dead ('my soul is not me'). That both of these are true supplies motives to both mourn *and* organise. Living in the times between the Kingdom's inauguration and its coming in its fullness, we cannot but grieve over our losses, and we must co-operate with God in bringing about the fullness of the Kingdom.

4.2 Remembering in the Light of Politics

If Marx's appeal to the text 'let the dead bury the dead' is psychologically flawed, it is also politically flawed, and politically flawed precisely from the perspective of a politics inspired by Marx. The memory of the dead is a vital impetus to political action and should not be excluded from liberative politics. We have already met Benjamin's view that such politics is motivated on the picture of enslaved forebears, 'not on the ideal of the emancipated heirs'. This is certainly true to political experience (an important exception seems to be contemporary environmental politics, which for obvious reasons makes constitutive appeal to the needs of *future* generations). Think here of the appeal of black liberationists to the history of slavery, of revolutionary nationalists (in Ireland, say) to the past wrongs of colonialism, of socialists to the past suffering and death of workers (the institution of Workers Memorial Day is a case in point here). But, granted that the dead play a role in contemporary liberative political life, that they are not simply to be abandoned, left to bury themselves, what *kind* of role do they play in present-day politics? And what are the theological ramifications of this? Benjamin writes,

> The conception of happiness, in other words, resonates irremediably with that of resurrection. It is just the same with the conception of the past, which makes history into its affair. The past carries a secret index with it, by which it is referred to its resurrection. Are we not touched by the same breath of air which was among that which came before? Is there not an echo of those who have been silenced in the voices to which we lend our ears today? Have not the women, who we court, sisters who they do not recognize anymore? If so, then there is a secret protocol between the generations of the past and that of our own. For we have been expected upon this earth. For it has been given us to know, just like every generation before us, a *weak* messianic power, on which the past has a claim. This claim is not to be settled lightly. The historical materialist knows why. (Benjamin [1940] 2005, Thesis II)

The theological resonances here cannot be missed. The past is 'referred to its resurrection'; we know 'a weak messianic power on which the past has a claim'. Here the hope of, in some sense, the redemption of the dead is held out in terms of their resurrection, and of the inauguration of the messianic age. Benjamin's secular, yet religiously inflected, Judaism is on full display in this passage, and forms a fascinating basis for dialogue with those concerned with political theology. However, it is precisely as *political* that Benjamin's attention to 'those who have been silenced' needs to be understood. It would be a mistake to read this passage as looking forward passively to some future redemption, after the fashion of a piously apolitical religious believer. The clue is in the final sentence, it is the historical materialist, the Marxist, who understands the messianic claim Benjamin wants to make. The redemption of the dead, as understood here is a political matter, to be fought for in history in the manner consist with a Marxist understanding of past and present, namely through the action of the working class.

The manner in which, according to Benjamin, the dead are to be redeemed is made clearer in another thesis from *On the Concept of History,*

> To articulate what is past does not mean to recognize 'how it really was.' It means to take control of a memory, as it flashes in a moment of danger. For historical materialism it is a question of holding fast to a picture of the past, just as if it had unexpectedly thrust itself, in a moment of danger, on the historical subject. The danger threatens the stock of tradition as much as its recipients. For both it is one and the same: handing itself over as the tool of the ruling classes. In every epoch, the attempt must be made to deliver tradition anew from the conformism which is on the point of overwhelming it. For the Messiah arrives not merely as the Redeemer; he also arrives as the vanquisher of the Anti-Christ. The only writer of history with the gift of setting alight the sparks of hope in the past, is the one who is convinced of this: that not even the dead will be safe from the enemy, if he is victorious. And this enemy has not ceased to be victorious. (Benjamin [1940] 2005, Thesis VI)

Here it is clear that Benjamin is concerned with the legacy of the dead, with their history, in the sense of the narrative of their past lives. There is no sense in which the dead are still with us. What is present to us, however, is a memory, a tradition. And this memory is not a fixed thing. It is readily made into the 'tool of the ruling class'. For this reason, in Benjamin's much-quoted words, 'not even the dead will be safe from the enemy'. Their legacy can be distorted, co-opted, or, for that matter, forgotten. The redemption of this legacy, again portrayed in messianic terms, is a setting free of 'tradition' from 'conformism', a ruling class conformism which is nothing less than the anti-Christ.

The conviction that not even the dead are safe under conditions of exploitation and oppression is a striking one, and it is worth recalling that these words were written in the face of a Nazi regime which was brutally re-narrating the history of *inter alia* the Jewish people. Yet, the point is a more general one: our capacity to remember the suffering of others itself occurs in a social context, and if that context becomes unfavourable our remembering can go awry. In spite of the dead being really dead, real harm can be done to them. It can go more or less well for a person after death depending on how their story is told. But if this is true, it is equally the case that things can go better for the dead under other social circumstances; their memory can be redeemed and so, in a certain sense, they themselves can be redeemed. Not that there is any sense for Benjamin that the dead are not really dead, rather it is precisely *as dead* that they are redeemed. The social struggle, then, is amongst other things a struggle for the dead, who are in danger from 'the enemy'.

So, for Benjamin, the dead are not simply beyond the political pale, as with Marx's 'let the dead bury the dead'. Instead, not only does the suffering of past generations provide a powerful motive for political struggle but also the dead themselves become an object of political contestation, with social struggles having amongst their purpose making the dead safe and redeeming their memory.

4.3 The Theological Consequences of a Politics of Remembrance

Much though Benjamin deploys theological tropes, indeed famously maintains that historical materialism can triumph in secret union with theology (Benjamin [1940] 2005, Thesis I), his is not a realist theistic position. His thoughts on the relationship of the dead to liberative politics are, however, compelling, and this raises the question of how a politically aware Christian theology ought to engage with them. What follows are some thoughts on this.

Benjamin's sense of the importance of memory resonates with the thought of Johann-Baptist Metz. He reminds his readers too of the importance of memory, specifically of what he terms 'dangerous memory' (Metz 2007) His primary focus is on the dangerous memory of Jesus Christ, who is not, of course, for Metz, as for mainstream Christian theology, dead. Nevertheless, even here there are parallels with Benjamin. The memory of Jesus, like Benjamin's memory of oppressed ancestors, spurs those who encounter it on to *praxis*. Moreover, the memory of Jesus is not simply a distanced remembering of the past, but an *anamnesis*, through which the past event of Jesus is made present. Now whilst Christian theologians will typically want to draw a distinction between the sense in which remembering Jesus renders him present, especially with respect to the

eucharistic memorial, and the manner in which remembering the dead represents some kind of encounter with them, there is a sense in Benjamin of the
present bleeding through into the past which could usefully be explored with
respect to Metz's ideas. One thing worth noticing is that the 'direction of travel'
in remembering seems frequently to be opposite in Benjamin and Metz: for
Metz, remembering brings the past into the present, whereas for Benjamin
remembering has an impact on the past, at least as narrativised. Yet it seems,
to me at least, that these are complementary positions, each shedding light on
the complex relationship between the remembered past and the political present.

It is also interesting to consider how a Benjaminian politics of remembrance
might sit alongside the account of an intermediate state that I sketched in
Section 3.2. Remember that on this account the soul is to be understood not as
an extra spiritual 'part' of the human person, still less as the 'real' person, but
rather as something like the person's narrative, as sustained by God. Now there
are obvious connections here with Benjamin's understanding of the politics of
remembrance. For this is also concerned with narrative, with how the stories of
the dead are told, and for that matter whether they are told at all. We, by political
action, can change how those stories are told, and so in a certain sense redeem
the dead.

One link to Christian eschatology which might seem obvious here is to the
doctrine of purgatory. Recall that I talked above about purgatory in terms of the
'editing' of a person's narrative. Isn't this precisely what is going on in political
action, understood in Benjaminian terms? A person, or better, some people, are
having their story retold in such a way that their sufferings are recognised, their
efforts acknowledged, their faults set in context. Against too easy a doctrinal
reconciliation here, it needs to be emphasised that traditionally purgatory has
been understood in terms of the healing of the *faults* of a person. It would be
a foolhardy thinker who didn't hold that we typically have culpabilities within
our narratives at the end of our lives, and that these stand in need of healing.
Focusing here on the individual case, however, we can surely admit that both
kinds of healing are needed post-mortem: the relational healing of a person's
narrative as it relates to socio-political situation, to being the victim of oppression, to having unfulfilled possibilities and frustrated projects, on the one hand,
and to the healing of those aspects of narrative in which a person has been at
fault, on the other. Both of kinds of healing, moreover, involve the way a person
has related to others during life – fractured and alienated relationships. So there
is much commonality between, what we might call, politico-historical healing
and more personal healing (the distinction here, of course, should not be
understood as in any way absolute: our personal faults are shot through with
our socio-political situation, and vice-versa).

One thing that is interesting about the idea that our socio-political narratives and politically inflected relationships can be renarrated in the sight of God after our death is that the political action of others seems to be integral to this renarration. It may be through a victorious revolution, for example, that a life can be vindicated and the seemingly final frustration of their hopes and desires under exploitative social conditions can be viewed as somehow redeemed. Note that for the Christian, but not for Benjamin, this redemption can be understood in realist terms: there is a real and lasting change in a person's narrative, guaranteed by the life of God and to be vindicated at the resurrection. Note, moreover, that the classical view that our actions (suffrages, works of mercy) can help the souls in purgatory receives here a radical extension: our political actions can bring about changes in those souls, understood in narrative terms.

A striking consequence of this is that the stories of the dead might be redeemed politically even after they have been 'edited' in such a way that all personal culpability has been transcended in the light of God's mercy. To put the point in old-fashioned terms, even souls in heaven can change, and can change for politically grounded reasons. This is certainly an unconventional conclusion; it has historically been thought that the souls in heaven, enjoying the Beatific Vision, stand beyond the need of any transformation. There has to be the suspicion, though, that this position belongs to the picture of heaven which we have already found reason to reject in the light of Marx, as a realm beyond the reach of politics. On the contrary, the dead, even the blessed dead, are the subjects of ongoing contestation, and will be until the Kingdom comes in its fullness.

The mention of the Kingdom is important here. Schillebeeckx (1987), a theologian whose work is thoroughly perfused with political consciousness, reminds us that, 'whilst everything is political, politics is not everything' (p. 78). For Christians, politics is not everything precisely because of the Kingdom. Whilst here and now everything is political – including, as we have seen, eschatology – when the fulfilment of our eschatological hope comes, all struggles for justice will be fulfilled, and there will be no more need for politics. In the end, not everything is political, even though in the here and now we cannot but see our Kingdom-orientated hope in political terms. Because of the Kingdom, ultimately politics is not everything.

It is the Kingdom, then, which represents the end-point of the transformation of the stories of the dead through social struggle. The Kingdom, remember, should be the central theme of Christian eschatology (and the intermediate state should *not* be this). So we look forward to the day when all our stories have been made into what God wills them to be. To quote an African American spiritual used as the title of an essay by Rowan Williams (2000), 'Nobody Knows Who

I Am 'Til Judgement Morning' (ch. 18). The unfulfilled hopes and unrealised capacities of the exploited down through the ages will be seen in a new light in the Kingdom.

This, of course, raises a familiar problem. Doesn't the Marxian critique of eschatology deserve to be re-asserted at this point? For if we can look forward to a future Kingdom in which we can be confident that our stories will be repaired, doesn't that dim the urgency of fighting to improve the stories that can be told about us in the present, and of struggling, in Benjaminian fashion, on behalf of the memory of the dead? On aspect of the answer here, as before, is to hold the Marxian critique in tension with eschatological belief, to never let the critique out of our sight, but to be constantly alert to the danger of our eschatology effecting reconciliation, modifying our proclamation and our practice if it appears to be functioning in this way. But another important aspect here relates to the active role of human agency in the theological politics of remembrance laid out above. The Kingdom is not something which arrives by divine imposition from above without the contribution of human agency. Rather, we struggle for the Kingdom. Our actions safeguard the memory of the dead, who without those actions are not safe from their enemies; our actions bring about justice, which will make future stories more adequate than many at present. So, if our focus is on the Kingdom, this, far from being a disincentive to political action, spurs on that action which will hasten the Kingdom.

This does not mean that the Kingdom is not sheer divine gift. As we have already had occasion to note, divine action and human action do not compete. One and the same reality can be brought about in part by human social struggle and by divine action at one and the same time. It should be added here that none of this implies the neo-Pelagian thesis that it is, on the side of human action, only political struggle which brings about the Kingdom. It is entirely open to the proponent of the time of thought supported here to hold, as I do, that the life, death, and resurrection of Jesus Christ are indispensable to the bringing out of the Kingdom. The work of *this particular* human being are of unique value, and the preservation of his memory (*anamnesis*) vital amongst all our memorialising. Yet, even here, I would want to draw connections to social struggle. In Christ the Kingdom is inaugurated, and all our works towards that Kingdom participate in his, who both establishes the Kingdom and uniquely signifies it.[53] The dangerous memory of Christ points forward to the day when we will all be remembered in the light of God's love and mercy, and our participation in social struggle is a real contribution to the dawning of that day.

---

[53] I have in mind here the conception of Christ himself as a sacrament. In a modern context this is developed by Schillebeeckx in his 1963.

5 Could It Be Worth It?

Eagleton writes,

> Even if there are those who are fortunate enough to disembark at the destin-
> ation of a just society, there remains the question of those who died in the
> tunnels and perished on the sidings – those who were not delivered by the
> engine of history into a felicitous terminus, but whose very names were
> expunged from the historical record, and who lived lives of such fruitless,
> back-breaking toil, that it might truly be asked in a Schopenhauerian spirit
> whether they would not have been better off never being born. What of the
> countless millions who have fallen by the wayside, unfulfilled and
> unremembered … It is striking how few Marxists appear to have asked
> themselves whether even the most resplendently emancipated future could
> outweigh this saga of sorrow. (Eagleton 2015, p. 36)

Marxism, for Eagleton, is a tragic outlook (in spite of Marx not viewing his own
ideas in this way). Even if communism is brought about, the waste and suffering of
past centuries will haunt the new society, and those who underwent these things,
however much there is a politics of remembering them, will not themselves enjoy
the fruit of the new society. And this is true even whilst it remains the case that past
injustices are precisely a powerful incentive for present day struggles.

Eagleton quotes Horkheimer, 'what has happened to the human beings who have
fallen no future can repair'.[54] If this is right, Marxism is indeed tragic. We might
very well fight for, and even obtain, a society which, if not perfect,[55] is a vast
improvement on other societies present and past, which is free from the kind of
structural features which resulted in the deaths of millions down through history,
but for all that we cannot bring back and compensate those who died in the course
of that history. A question hangs over anyone who would improve society (so, not
just the Marxist): what is the value of our potential achievement in the face of the
horrendous ills to which our fellow human beings have been subject over the
centuries? Wouldn't political victory ring hollow in the light of these?[56]

These questions are not, in Eagleton's asking of them at least, supposed to
dissuade us from engaging in liberative praxis, or even to relativise our com-
mitment to that praxis. However, the questions haunt – or should haunt – anyone

---

[54] Quoted in Lowy 2005, p. 31.

[55] Against the more utopian readings of the Marxist tradition, we must surely insist that there is no
perfect society to be had (at least this side of the *eschaton*). The Marxist claim about communism
is not that it would be perfect but rather that it would be free from systematic and structural
exploitation and oppression.

[56] Note that what is not being presented here is a request for a theodicy, or even for a secular
equivalent of a theodicy (whatever that might involve). I am profoundly sceptical of the project
of theodicy (Kilby 2020). But once we have set aside the theodicial project, there remains an
existential question: what are our achievements in the face of so much suffering?

who is involved in trying to improve human society. For even if we succeed in doing that, there is so much we cannot repair, because it lies in the past, in graves. It is true, as we have seen, that there is a sense in which political action can redeem the past, but what it cannot do is revive the dead and allow them a taste of those goods so many of them were denied in their lifetimes. Still less can it offer them recompense for the evil with which they were afflicted. This being so, any political victory, whilst worthwhile, will be tinged with tragedy, burdened by the memories, where there are memories, of the dead, and burdened as well by the knowledge that there are millions of dead now forgotten. No amount of flourishing in a future free society can eliminate this burden.

But now consider the case of a Christian committed to political struggle. Is she bound to resign herself to her endeavours having a tragic quality? Christianity, after all, makes claims about final redemption. Might those claims speak to the problematic laid out by Eagleton? On the face of it the Christian might be thought to have resources to speak to the phenomenon of pointless death down through the ages.[57] There is an immediate danger of a Christian response here that is glib, not doing sufficient homage to the weight of suffering down through the centuries. There is a proper reverence in the face of death. However, the Christian theologian dares to profess nevertheless that there is a sense in which death is defeated, 'where O death is your victory? Where O death is your sting?'[58] The theological challenge is twofold: to articulate this defeat in a way that avoids sitting lightly to the reality of historical loss, and to apply that articulation to the themes which Eagleton raises. This must be done, moreover, in a way that is humble and suitably cautious in the wake of the subject matter, not least because the Marxian critique of religion lies in wait for any theological response to that subject matter, as we will see.

5.1 What Can Christianity Say?

The Book of Revelation offers a vision of the defeat of death and the end of mourning:

> He will wipe every tear from their eyes.
> Death will be no more;
> mourning and crying and pain will be no more,
> for the first things have passed away.[59]

---

[57] She might also be thought to face an additional problem, that of the problem of evil. I am unsympathetic here, and side with Davies in press, in holding that the problem of evil rests on a category mistake.

[58] 1 Corinthians 15:55.   [59] Revelation 21:4.

The text is often used the context of funerals and other occasions of memorial, and has been a source of great comfort for many people down through the centuries. Given our engagement with Marx, however, we cannot assume lightly that being a source of comfort is ideologically neutral. We should interrogate whether the comfort being offered is genuine and, more to the Marxian point, examine how it functions, to see whether an ultimately undesirable reconciliation is being effected.

That said, this is a work of Christian theology, and with that in view I must emphasise that I myself cannot but draw comfort from the quoted passage and from the ideas with which it has resonated down through centuries of interpretation and liturgical use. The project of this Element is to read the Christian tradition on eschatology alongside a Marxian critique of eschatology. Our focus here will be on how Christian theology can respond to the subject of this section – the countless millions of lives and deaths passed in suffering and pointlessness – that is, how theology might be able to speak to an intra-Marxist concern.

The outlines of what a Christian theologian has to say will be familiar enough. The Eagletonian worry which is our present concern is one about death, specifically the deaths of millions of ordinary people, often in anonymous poverty, down through history. Death, however – so claims Christianity – is defeated. Or rather, in a way that echoes, and not without reason, the way things are with respect to the Kingdom: the defeat of death has been inaugurated through the resurrection of Jesus, and will be established fully at the end of all things. 'The last enemy to be destroyed is death.'[60]

What does it mean to say that death is, and will be, defeated? The Pauline assertion that death is to be destroyed occurs in the context of a discussion of the resurrection of the dead. Christ has been raised, and this is the first blow to be struck against death, and we, too, shall be raised, this bringing to fulfilment the destruction of death. We have already seen how the doctrine of the resurrection of the dead represents an improvement on the popular dualistic picture of an afterlife. Now we are suggesting, on behalf of Christian theology in conversation with Marxism, that the resurrection of the dead provides an ultimate vindication of the exploited and oppressed down through history. This is not, it is important to emphasise, a vindication of their sufferings; rather, it is a vindication of the people who have undergone those sufferings, the revelation that death does not have the last word in their lives. Of course, this is not to say that death has not seemed to reign supreme over their historical lives, that grotesque amounts of harm have been done to human beings by their fellows,

---

[60] 1 Corinthians 15:26.

or that thousands have not fallen in what was for them a futile struggle for a better world. Nothing Christianity has to say undoes the tragic nature of Marxism. This is because Marxism is concerned with events in human history. Christianity, however, talks about realities which transcend[61] human history – the resurrection of the dead and the Kingdom of God – and as such is in a position to offer an afterword to this tragedy.

The point is not that Christianity undoes historic harms; these persist as part of the stories of human lives just as much as the wounds persist on the body of the Risen Christ. Nor is the point that Christianity offers compensation for these harms, as though there were some kind of transaction between God and history. The point is not even that a theodicy is being offered; this, to my mind, would represent an offensive instrumentalism concerning the historic sufferings under consideration.[62] Rather, what the resurrection of the dead consists in is death not having the last word. The redeemed find that their stories end up in a state of fellowship with one another and with God, the God whose Son also endured historic wrongs yet found new life in the resurrection.

All of this, even once the necessary qualifications have been made, might sound too upbeat. So it is important to be clear: what is being presented is not a straightforward claim that Christian theology has an answer to the question of tragedy in Marxism, or rather that Christian theology has such an answer that it should confidently assert when faced with a Marxist troubled by this question. I do indeed hold that Christianity has something vitally important to say about the, hard-won and ultimate, destiny of the dead. But the simple assertion of this to someone grappling with the truth that history is, from many perspectives, a pile of corpses will ring hollow. It is only from the perspective of shared struggle, and of shared confrontation of the death and defeat which precedes, and too often follows from, struggle, that the Christian can make a tentative suggestion that she has a vision which redeems, but does not undo, the history in question.

5.2 But Is Christianity Tragic?

Christianity, then, offers hope, not a shallow or an easy hope, but a hope nonetheless. This poses a question about the nature of eschatology. When we consider the eschatological hope offered by Christian faith, the query arises: is Christianity, then, tragic or comic (in the traditional sense of these terms)?

---

[61] Transcend in the Hegelian-Marxist sense of *aufheben* – the resurrection and Kingdom are not extra-historical in the sense that heaven is on the tempting dualistic picture. Rather they lie beyond history, through fulfilling it. Hence, amongst other things, the language of the 'last day'.

[62] Against the very project of theodicy from a politically engaged perspective see Surin 1986. For a subtly different view, still resistant to the provision of theodicy, see Kilby 2020, ch. 6.

Eagleton comes down firmly on the side of Christianity possessing a tragic outlook. He argues this at several points in his work, as for that matter does theologian Jessica Coblentz (2020). Perhaps most clearly, Eagleton promotes the idea just after the passage quoted earlier,

> George Steiner, for whom any vigorous faith in humanity spells the ruin of tragedy, argues in The Death of Tragedy that neither Marxism nor Christianity can be classed as a tragic creed. 'The least touch of any theology that has a compensating Heaven to offer the tragic hero is fatal',[63] he insists. He is thinking, however, of these doctrines' affirmative visions of the future, not of the alarmingly steep price one has to pay for them. Resurrection does not cancel the reality of crucifixion, or communism the horrors of class society. Indeed, one might claim that part of what disappears when the Christian doctrine of hope becomes the secular ideology of progress is precisely its tragic dimension. (Eagleton 2015, pp. 36–7)

Christian hope certainly loses something when it is transformed into a secular ideology of progress, and part of what it loses is the realisation that our ultimate destiny, the Kingdom of God, comes about by means of a path that passes through the Cross, and through the innumerable sufferings borne by the Kingdom's future inhabitants. The question is, however, whether being in possession of this realisation renders Christianity tragic. Eagleton's affirmative answer here draws on his more general account of tragedy. At the outset of a significant work on the topic, Eagleton says, 'it may well turn out that "very sad" . . . is about the best we can do when it comes to . . . tragic art' (2003b, p. 1). His point is that the ordinary use of the word 'tragedy' is to indicate occurrences which *are* very sad, heartrending even. He never abandons this quotidian account of tragedy, but goes on to examine the tragic in art, and to argue forcibly that we ignore it at our peril, because in so doing we turn our eyes from the realities of pain, suffering and injustice. Confronting these in the form of art reminds us of their persisting reality in human life, and therefore both speaks to us and (sometimes)[64] spurs us on to action.

What, then, about Christianity? The Christian story certainly contains tragic elements; we are reminded of these every time we see a crucifix, or work to alleviate the suffering of the dispossessed and the hurting. But the question remains whether Christianity is *ultimately* tragic – tragic in the older sense in which whatever it is that has harmed the protagonist, or

---

[63] I have in mind here the idea that Christ is a *sacrament* of the Kingdom (as, I think, in a different way, is the Church, but arguing this is for another place.)

[64] The qualification is important for Eagleton. Some tragic occurrences are beyond our political agency, contrary to the apparent insistences of enthusiastic left historicisers. The most obvious example is death.

protagonists, persists unresolved at the end of the story. In this sense
Christianity is not tragic, which is – as we have already seen – not to
ignore the reality of pain on the way to the Kingdom, nor to claim that
tragic elements, in the Eagletonian sense, don't persist in the stories of the
Kingdom's inhabitants.

In fact these elements, and in particular peoples' experiences of depressive suffering, motivate Coblentz (2020) to move that Christianity is tragic.
She is certainly correct to draw her readers' attention to suffering of
a magnitude and persistence such that we ought to hastily expect it to be
swept away by the tide of redemption. The truth is that we do not know,
and cannot imagine, how God will heal some harms. In this sense Coblentz
is surely right, Christianity contains tragic elements, and if we take that as
sufficient for its being tragic (as Eagleton seems to), then in that sense
Christianity is tragic. That I do not want to deny. I do, however, want to
deny that Christianity is tragic in the same sense as Marxism. Christianity
has a story of ultimate redemption which is, at least potentially, universal
in scope. Marxism, for all that it holds out a needful hope for political
transformation in the present, does not.

It cannot be emphasised enough that none of this negates the real horrors
suffered by human beings down through history. What is being claimed is that
the Kingdom is the end of the stories of history's inhabitants, and that this is
a good end, in spite of the very real, and often inexplicable, horrors on the road
to that Kingdom. In particular, without justifying or setting aside, the oppression and lived futility of countless millions down through the ages, those
millions this section began by acknowledging, we can hope that they, too,
might be resurrected into the Kingdom. Christianity is penultimately tragic
but ultimately comic.

5.3 Marxism and Tragedy

What, then, about Marxism'? Does it provide a tragic outlook on human
existence. It might seem not. The hope Marx has in the unleashed potential
for human flourishing under communism[65] is palpable and exciting. The
Communist Manifesto ends, 'The Proletarians have nothing to lose but their
chains. They have a world to win' (Marx and Engels 1848). The nature of life in
the world which the working class has to win had been described earlier in *The
German Ideology*,

---

[65] It must be emphasised that communism, for Marx, who was amongst other things a critic of the
state, is a very different form of society from that realised in the former Eastern Bloc or in
contemporary China.

In communist society, where nobody has one exclusive sphere of activity but each can become accomplished in any branch he wishes, society regulates the general production and thus makes it possible for me to do one thing today and another tomorrow, to hunt in the morning, fish in the afternoon, rear cattle in the evening, criticise after dinner, just as I have a mind, without ever becoming hunter, fisherman, herdsman or critic. (Marx and Engels 1845)

Now this cannot be accepted as it is. There is an irreducible need for skill in some tasks, and our opportunity to obtain certain skills is frustrated by our finitude, regardless of the existence of a rigid social division of labour or the imposition of waged work. Nevertheless, Marx hoped for a world in which human capacities were given far more room to find fulfilment than under capitalism, and in that hope some of us still join him. Isn't this vision far from tragic? If one hopes that history comes to a point where human beings can manifest their capacities maximally, then what one hopes for is surely precisely the opposite of tragedy.

For all that hope for a better future pervades Marxian thought, however, this divesting it of tragic status is too quick. This is for the reasons outlined by Eagleton in the passage quoted at the start of this section. Whilst those who come to live in a communist society, as envisaged by Marx (and it bears repeating that what Marx means by 'communism' is far removed from the societies of the former Eastern Bloc), will, according to him, flourish and have their human nature fulfilled, there are untold millions who have lived before-hand and have been denied this opportunity. The point generalises to other forms of emancipatory politics. Suppose that feminism is successful in abolish-ing patriarchy. It remains the case that centuries of forced marriage, of rape, of violence, and of discrimination hang over countless, now dead, women. And these legacies of oppression and exploitation sit uncomfortably alongside the liberated futures to which they lead. Even though *some* people come to enjoy the fruits of emancipation, many others didn't. What about them? It is in the light of this question that we should affirm that Marxism is indeed tragic. Even if its aim is fulfilled, and a society conducive to human flourishing is brought about, still there are stories – unredeemed in Marxism's own terms – to which there seems to be no joyful ending, stories of agony and destitution, of the frustration of hopes and desires and of the simple denial of humanity. This is surely tragedy if anything is.

A response might be made in a Benjaminian vein. Those we are identifying as tragic victims within the Marxian framework are precisely the 'enslaved fore-bears' on whose behalf, according to Benjamin, people in the present engage in struggle. When that struggle is victorious surely, our Benjaminian interlocutor can be imagined continuing, there is a real sense in which the dead victims of history are redeemed. For a start, they stand vindicated, against those who might have professed their suffering to be an historical necessity, their oppression to be part of the natural order of things. Then again, their story can now be told as part of a narrative which leads to the negation of the structures under which they suffered and died, and this, as we have seen, lends a new quality to the ways in which they are remembered.

There is much to be said in favour of the Benjaminian response. What it claims is true, and forms the basis for a politics of the dead, with the potential to be shared by religious believer and non-believer alike. It is just that there is a clear perspective from which the response doesn't offer enough to history's victims. They remain dead, and never lived to experience the better future which followed on from their deaths. It was never manifest *for them*, and for all that they knew the kind of sufferings they endured were a permanent part of history. Many of them will have died, not only unfulfilled, but also without hope. Here is the inalienable tragedy in the Marxist view of the world.

5.4 Christianity Speaking to Marxism

Marxism is tragic. Christianity is, at the last turn, comic. Is there a perspective from which Christianity might embrace Marxism and lend it the resources to transcend tragedy? I have argued elsewhere (Hewitt 2020) that Marxism and Christianity are compatible, so there seems to be the basis for a positive answer. The question moreover is general in its importance; it is not only Marxism but feminism, black liberation, any movement which seeks to transcend historic injustice which is tragic in exactly the manner we saw with Marxism. Anything we say about Marxism and tragedy, then, can be said about those movements as well.

The proposal is a straightforward one. Christianity puts forward the hope of redemption after death, of resurrection into the Kingdom where all our struggles for justice find completion and all will live well in a 'new heavens and a new earth'. Cannot this vision be put forward to the Marxist and so, whilst not stemming her tears over the carnage of history, offer a genuine hope on behalf of history's victims, thus rendering her vision ultimately non-tragic?

I think the answer here is positive, and so we can, having thus far avoided any such suggestion, propose that Christianity has something to offer Marxism. What it has to offer is precisely hope in the face of death, a hope that we cannot help but feel is needed for the millions of anonymous dead, and a hope which Marxism on its own cannot supply. But now we are in a strange position, given what has gone before in this Element. It has been a constant refrain up until this point that Christianity ought to take seriously the Marxian critique of its afterlife belief, and in particular ought not to be quick to offer the prospect of beatitude hereafter in compensation for worldly misery. Yet isn't this precisely what I am proposing now? Admittedly I have talked in terms of the Kingdom, and the hereafter being envisaged is non-dualistically conceived and continuous with this-worldly struggles for justice. However it is a hereafter for all that, and it is being intimately related to evils done to suffering human beings in this world. Once again, aren't we back to 'the opium of the people'?

One thing that can be said here is that there is a distinction to be made between the function of afterlife belief with respect to past human beings and that of afterlife belief with respect to present human beings. It is with respect to the latter that the charge of providing reconciliatory compensation most obviously hits home. But what if Benjamin is right, and our struggles for justice are, in an important sense, in the name of and on behalf of the dead of the past? Isn't there a danger that believing that those dead will come to enjoy the fullness of God's Kingdom will remove an incentive to struggle on their behalf, namely that the only way they can be in any sense redeemed is through present day struggles?

There should be no doubt that this is a danger. However, the theme of the relationship between divine agency and human struggles is one that has recurred throughout this Element, and I will repeat here what I have said before. There is no competition between God's action and our action. We are not on the same metaphysical level, such that the agency of one can 'get in the way' of the other. In particular, our struggles for justice and God's bringing in of the Kingdom are not exclusive alternatives. It can remain, then, entirely the case that we work the redemption of the historic dead through struggling for their vindication even while that struggle is part of God's act which ultimately ushers in the Kingdom which those dead will enjoy for all eternity.

But we can too quickly say such things whilst in practice being stuck in a state of mind and action for which eschatology functions like opium. However much we may be in theory committed to the resurrection of the body and to a Kingdom built, in part, out of our political agency, eschatology might still feature in our lives as a too-easy consolation. It might become a way of evading harsh realities, even when our official position is that those realities ought to be confronted. Now, doesn't this cast doubt on whether what the Christian is offering the Marxist is a blessing or a curse? Might she not be proposing something which will have the effect of stripping the Marxist of transformative energy?

This risk has to be kept constantly in mind. My theme up until this point is that Christianity has to learn, in humility, from Marx. It would be to carelessly set aside that insight to at this point say that the Christian should ride roughshod over Marxist concerns and hastily propose an afterlife as the ultimate solution to the riddle of history. And yet Christianity does contain an eschatology and understands it as a source of hope. There is a tension here between taking the Marxian critique of afterlife belief seriously, on the one hand, and recognising the genuine and universal hope contained in Christian eschatology, on the other. My view is that this is a tension that needs to be lived with. Our eschatology should be constantly and deeply examined in the light of Marx's critique, whilst our activism should keep before it the hope that is held out for all of creation, past, present, and future. We will feel a tension at points between these two imperatives, but it has the potential to be a creative tension. It is, moreover, part of the wider tension that issues from living at a time when the Kingdom is inaugurated but not fully realised.

But why should Marxists care at all about Christian truth-claims?[66] The Marxist's first concern, as we have seen, is not with the *truth* (or otherwise) of Christian beliefs, but with their *function*? The problem a Marxist has with belief in an afterlife is not that it is false (although a typical Marxist will certainly hold that it is), but rather that it serves to reconcile the exploited and oppressed to their exploitation and oppression. Taking on board the danger of her belief effecting such a reconciliation, the Christian theologian may insist nonetheless that a reason for taking her truth claims seriously is that they are *true*! As long as this is not asserted in too bold a mode or arrogantly, this has something going for it. The Christian believes something important is true, the (typical) Marxist doesn't; the Christian has motive to encourage the Marxist to share her belief. But there are reasons specific to the Marxist why she ought to be concerned with Christian truth-claims. For the Marxist is not concerned with functionality in a purely mechanical way; she is not merely a sociologist. Her ultimate concern is with human liberation. And it is here that Christian claims could capture her interest. What hope is there, this section has asked, for those who have died without political liberation? The Christian claims, albeit that she should, in my view, do so quietly and sensitively, that there is hope for these dead. There is a form of liberation which continues beyond political liberation and encompasses the dead of centuries. And that, if true, is a claim worth hearing.

5.5 Christian and Marxist Eschatology?

So, if what has been said up until this point is correct, the Marxist would benefit from taking on board Christian eschatology (which, to make my position explicit, cannot coherently be done without taking on board Christianity more generally), but the Christian should be profoundly careful about suggesting this,

---

[66] Thank you to two anonymous reviewers for pushing me on this question.

continually examining and refining her position in the light of Marx's critique. One influential writer on Christianity and Marx, Nicholas Lash, understood the relationship between Marx and Christian eschatology differently from this, and his stance is worth considering briefly.

In his *A Matter of Hope* (1981), Lash reads Marx (and, by extension, the Marxist tradition) as possessing its own eschatology, having human perfection as its *telos*. So, writes Lash, 'Christianity, like Marxism, looks forward to the total redemption of humanity' (1981, p. 278). The claim that Marxism looks forward to 'the total redemption of humanity' is a striking one, and one for which I can find no evidence in the Marxian corpus or in the writings of most subsequent Marxists. This is just as well for the Marxist, since the suggestion that humanity's total redemption can be obtained through the methods of Marxism is wholly unbelievable, not least for the Eagletonian reasons assayed earlier. But it is worth registering Lash's view that there is an irreducible sense in which Christianity and Marxism are rivals. On the contrary, however, I do not think that Marxism contains anything like an eschatology, but altogether more modestly it hopes for an ending of class society. That hope does not warrant being described as eschatological in anything other than a metaphorical sense.

Hope, as the title of his book suggests, is important to Lash. For him, 'hope consists in the refusal to succumb to either of the twin temptations of optimism or despair' (1981, p. 270). Lash's understanding, which is not the only understanding of optimism and despair is summed up well in the following passage, 'Despair surrenders the future; optimism sacrifices the present. The precariousness of hope arises from its refusal to tolerate either of these destructive "renunciations"' (1981, p. 277). This sitting lightly to future and present, respectively, issues, according to Lash, from a claim to know how the future will be (1981, pp. 271–2). But this simply doesn't follow. I might very well think that I know how the future will be without devaluing the present (or the future). After all it might well be that the future is to be built out of the present, such that the way in the present time to do justice to the future. Something like this is held by both Christianity and Marxism. It is the body with which I love and live in the present moment that is the seed of my life in the Kingdom; it is out of the present alienation of the working class that a liberated future becomes possible.

There is, for all, this something right about Lash's counselling of a reticence about optimism. And such a view is so pervasive, in liberal academia at least, that it deserves a hearing. However, there is a difference between the kind of reticence which I have urged in this Element: a preparedness to subject oneself to perpetual critique, and the bolder position that one doesn't know anything about the future. As it happens, I think Marx at his best does in fact disavow knowledge of the political future, his occasional lapses into what looks like determinism notwithstanding. With Christianity, though, the situation is more complicated. Paul's argument in 1 Corinthians 15, for example, is precisely that our belief about the eschatological future is grounded in the resurrection of Christ. Such belief, for Paul, is not simply a free-floating optimism, but nor is there not a sense in which it constitutes knowledge. After all, laying out the practical impact of resurrection belief, Paul tells the Corinthians 'you know that in the Lord your labour is not in vain'.[67]

Knowledge claims can make us nervous, and it is an implication of what has gone before here that we should not make them too quickly, or at least that we should not be too sure that we understand their content without a considerable amount of critique and collective soul-searching. However, there is knowledge that liberates as well as oppresses, and those of us who are Western academics, whose business it is to interrogate claims to knowledge, should not forget that our situation is a privileged one. In the rubble of a bombed house; in the wake of the terror of a death squad – these situations are, at least for the victims, beyond political redemption. In these situations the assertion that we know that our Redeemer lives, and that we will see him in our flesh,[68] can be more than a comfort, it can provide an insight into the truth of how things stand with eschatology. And, as I have argued, this needn't be an ideological move, reconciling those who remain to the horrors of what has gone before.

6 Conclusion

Karl Barth (1925), in a work written after his second *Romans* commentary, engages with the question of death. He has this to say,

> Let us not deceive ourselves: all our contemporaries stand in angst and need before the closed wall of death, hardly aware of the new thing which waits behind it, and we do not help with our speculative constructions and evangelistic or social busyness ... For the sake of the suffering of millions, for the sake of the forgotten blood of many, for the sake of the fear of the Lord, not that! If any word needs substantiation, attestation and realisation through corresponding ethical, social and political action it is the biblical saying that death is swallowed up in victory. (p. 92; translated Gorringe 1999, p. 53)

Barth is writing after the carnage of the First World War and his words speak to that context. They much more generally challenge Christians seeking to proclaim that death is swallowed up in victory[69] in the face of human misery, of wasted lives, of oppression and of exploitation. That proclamation cannot be made lightly in a way which diminishes the real suffering of the ages. As we

---

[67] 1 Corinthians 15:58.　　[68] Job 19: 25–6.　　[69] 1 Corinthians 15:54.

have seen, this serves to effect a too-speedy reconciliation and in doing so serves the interests precisely of those who exploit and oppress. The promise of heaven in the future can so easily draw attention away from earth now. Yet the proclamation remains to be made – death *is* swallowed up in victory; it does not have the last word in history.

The project of this Element has been to engage with Marx, and latterly with Marxism, as remedies against the Christian eschatological proclamation becoming too blasé or reconciliatory. In particular the Marxian critique acts as a brake, as it were, on the kind of preaching of the empty tomb which doesn't proceed by means of the Cross. There is a way of talking about the promises of Christianity which doesn't do justice to the suffering of human beings. Because it both sits lightly to that suffering and because it talks of future happiness, this way of talking is prone to function ideologically, reconciling people with things to which they ought not to be reconciled. There is a discipline in subjecting ourselves to the Marxian critique. In doing so, we are forced to check the content and impact of our words about eschatology. Nor is this process of holding ourselves accountable to Marx one that has an ending. We are constantly in danger in a society such as our own of articulating our religion in an ideological fashion. This is particularly true, I think, of eschatology. If we do not want this danger to be realised, critical voices need to be taken on board. And Marx's is prominent amongst those critical voices.

However, to return to a theme with which we began, I do not want merely to claim that reconciliatory accounts of an afterlife are unhelpful, ideological and conciliatory. It might be thought, after all, that there is logical space for them to be all of these things but still to be *true*. I want to resist this line of thought, by insisting that as well as being injurious to social transformation, reconciliatory accounts are *false*. This is because we know that God has been authoritatively revealed as being on the side of human justice, and therefore of the poor and oppressed. God wills to liberate these, and indeed it is the mark of the true God that God liberates, the gods who perpetuate oppression (McCabe 2002, p 32). We mean several things in calling God 'true', but one of them is that there are truths concerning God such that if we fail to acknowledge those truths we are, in some sense, recognising something less than God, a god. As we have learned from liberation theology, prominent amongst the truths definitive of God is that God liberates. It follows that claims which make God's action incompatible with liberation are false. Now, were God to bring about a heaven, belief in which inevitably diverted people from earthly liberation, it would be the case that God's action (in this respect) was incompatible with liberation. We can conclude that God has brought about no such heaven.

In the name of God and of truth, as well as of the exploited and the oppressed, then, we should oppose reconciliatory eschatologies. This does not mean that we have no eschatology left to proclaim. A central part of the work of this Element has been to sketch eschatological positions which, whilst still requiring to be read constantly and critically in the company of Marx, seem to avoid the most obviously devastating lines of Marxist criticism of Christian eschatologies. I argued for a reorientation of Christian eschatological hope, away from a dualistically conceived heaven, towards a focus on the resurrection of the body and the Kingdom of God. However, I also made a proposal for recovering an intermediate state, through appeal to a conception of the soul understood narratively. This allows the classical structure of Christian eschatology to be preserved within a framework which is sensitive to the force of Marx's critique.

The project of reconciling Marxist critique with orthodox Christianity might be thought to be yet another example of a reconciliation which serves injurious social purposes. For aren't Christian orthodoxy and the churches which cling to it prime examples of ideological structures upholding an unjust society? Certainly a good number of radical theologians have thought so, both breaking with orthodoxy at various points and, increasingly it seems to me, leaving the churches altogether. The charge is a serious one. My strategy in this Element has been simply to try to show, in one area, that it needn't be the case that Christian belief with a mainstream shape possesses an ideological character.[70] Of course, and as I have argued, that belief needs to be subject to perpetual critical scrutiny. But that is true of all theology: orthodox or otherwise; radical or otherwise.

The conclusion of this brief survey of a certain terrain is, then, that Christian eschatology ought to be subject to perpetual criticism in the light of Marx. But criticism is not the same thing as falsification. The Christian tradition contains within itself the resources to respond to that critique, albeit falteringly and with humility. It can emphasise the themes of the Kingdom and the resurrection of the body in a way that undermines dualistic and reconciliatory eschatologies. It can, moreover, recover a doctrine of the intermediate state in a manner which avoids dualism and is continuous with the reality of struggles against earthly injustice. The Christian hope for the dead therefore remains alive. That hope – as expressed in theology, in preaching, and in practice – should however be constantly interrogated to ensure that it is not tacitly functioning in a reconciliatory fashion.

This dialectic between Christian hope and Marxist criticism has been a recurrent theme in this Element. The two can work together, albeit not without tension, each one checking the other: Christianity offsetting the tragic nature of

---

[70] This formulation of my position ought not to be taken as implying that I am on board with the project known as radical orthodoxy. For my views on this, see Hewitt 2016.

Marxism; Marxism undermining the ideological nature of so much Christianity. One thing both have in common is a belief that the world as it is fails to be everything that it could be. For Christians, the world will come to be the Kingdom. For Marxists, it may yield a liberated society. Both think about this future in a way which includes the dead. Christianity holds that the dead will be resurrected into the Kingdom. Marxism, at least in its Benjaminian articulation, thinks that a liberated society will vindicate the dead of past ages. We have reason, on both accounts, to hope for ourselves in a way which involves the dead in our hope. Both we and the dead are on our way somewhere, somewhere we have not yet arrived. 'For here we have no enduring city, but we are looking for the city that is to come.'[71]

---

[71] Hebrews 13:14.

References

Augustine. 2012. *The Confessions*. Translated by Maria Boulding. San Francisco, Ignatius Press. (*Confessions*).

Balthasar, Hans Urs von. 1988. *Dare We Hope That All Men Will Be Saved? With a Short Discourse on Hell*. San Francisco, Ignatius Press.

Barth, Karl. 1925. *Das Wort Gott und die Theologie*. Munich, Kaiser.

Barth, Karl. 2001. *Protestant Theology in the Nineteenth Century: Its Background and History*. London, SCM Press.

Benjamin, Walter. (1940) 2005. *On the Concept of History*. Translated by Dennis Redmond. www.marxists.org/reference/archive/benjamin/1940/history.htm.

Coblentz, Jessica. 2020. 'Depressive Suffering as Tragic Suffering: Theological Insights and Trajectories' in Karen Kilby and Rachel Davies (eds.), *Suffering and the Christian Life*. Edinburgh, T&T Clark, pp. 155–62.

Corrin, Jay P. 2013. *Catholic Progressives in England after Vatican II*. Notre Dame, Notre Dame Press.

Davies, Brian. In press. 'Does the Problem of Evil Rest on a Mistake?' in *International Journal of Philosophy and Theology*.

Dyke, Christina van. 2012. 'I See Dead People: Disembodied Souls and Aquinas' "Two Person Problem"' in John Marebon (ed.), *Oxford Studies in Medieval Philosophy*. Oxford, Oxford University Press, pp. 25–45.

Eagleton, Terry. 2003a. *After Theory*. Harmondsworth, Penguin.

Eagleton, Terry. 2003b. *Sweet Violence: The Idea of the Tragic*. Oxford, Blackwell.

Eagleton, Terry. 2006. 'Lunging, Flailing, Mispunching' in *London Review of Books* 28(20). www.lrb.co.uk/the-paper/v28/n20/terry-eagleton/lunging-flailing-mispunching.

Eagleton, Terry. 2010. *Reason, Faith and Revolution: Reflections on the God Debate*. New Haven, Yale University Press.

Eagleton, Terry. 2015. *Hope without Optimism*. New Haven, Yale University Press.

Feuerbach, Ludwig. (1843) 1972. *The Essence of Christianity*. Second edition. Translated by Zawar Hanfi. www.marxists.org/reference/archive/feuerbach/works/essence/index.htm.

Freud, Sigmund. (1917) 1952. *Mourning and Melancholia*. Standard Edition of the Complete Psychological Works of Sigmund Freud, volume 14. London, Hogarth Press.

Gebara, Ivone and Bingemer, Maria Clara. 1989. *Mary, Mother of God, Mother of the Poor*. Maryknoll, Orbis.

Gorringe, Timothy. 1999. *Karl Barth: Against Hegemony.* Oxford, Oxford University Press.

Gutiérrez, Gustavo. 1996. *Selected Writings.* Edited by James B. Nickoloff. London, SCM.

Hewitt, Simon. 2016. 'Review of Adrian Pabst, "Metaphysics: the Creation of Hierarchy"' in *Journal of Theological Studies* 69(10), pp. 399–404.

Hewitt, Simon. 2020. *Church and Revolution: Continuing the Conversation between Christianity and Marxism.* Durham, Sacristy Press.

Hewitt, Simon. 2022. 'Aquinas on the Immortality of the Soul: Some Reflections' in *Heythrop Journal* 64(1), pp. 30–45.

Hewitt, Simon. 2024. 'McCabe on Marx' in *International Journal of Philosophy and Theology* 85(1–2), pp. 69–79.

Hill, Joe. 1911. *The Preacher and the Slave.* Folk song.

Insole, Christopher. 2004. *The Politics of Human Frailty: A Theological Defence of Political Liberalism.* London, SCM.

Jones, Peter E. 2018. 'Karl Marx and the Language Sciences: Critical Encounters – Introduction to the Special Issue' in *Language Sciences* 70,, pp. 1–15.

Kee, Alistair. 1990. *Marx and the Failure of Liberation Theology.* London, SCM.

Kerr, Fergus. 1997. *Theology after Wittgenstein.* Second edition. London, SPCK.

Kilby, Karen. 2020. *God, Evil and the Limits of Theology.* London, T&T Clark.

Klass, Dennis and Steffen, Edith (eds.). 2018. *Continuing Bonds in Bereavement: New Directions in Research and Practice.* London, Routledge.

Klopenborg, John S. and Verheyden, Joseph (eds.). 2014. *The Elijah-Elisha Narrative in the Composition of Luke.* Edinburgh, T&T Clark.

Lash, Nicholas. 1981. *A Matter of Hope: A Theologian's Reflections on the Thought of Karl Marx.* London, Darton, Longman & Todd.

Leech, Kenneth. 2001. *Through Our Long Exile: Contextual Theology and Urban Experience.* London, Darton, Longman & Todd.

Lennon, Kathleen. 2019. 'Feminist Perspectives on the Body', in Edward N. Zalta (ed.), *The Stanford Encyclopedia of Philosophy* (Fall 2019 edition). https://plato.stanford.edu/archives/fall2019/entries/feminist-body/.

Lowy, Michael. 2005. *Fire Alarm: Reading Walter Benjamin's 'On the Concept of History'.* London, Verso.

Marx, Karl. (1843) 2003. *On the Jewish Question.* www.marxists.org/archive/marx/works/1844/jewish-question/.

Marx, Karl. (1844) 1970. *Critique of Hegel's Philosophy of Right: Introduction.* Translated by Joseph O'Malley. www.marxists.org/archive/marx/works/download/Marx_Critique_of_Hegels_Philosophy_of_Right.pdf.

Marx, Karl. (1845) 2002. *Theses on Feuerbach.* Translated by Cyril Smith. www.marxists.org/archive/marx/works/1845/theses/index.htm.

Marx, Karl. (1852) 1937. *The Eighteenth Brumaire of Louis Bonaparte.* Moscow, Progress Press. www.marxists.org/archive/marx/works/1852/18th-brumaire/.

Marx, Karl and Engels, Friedrich. (1845) 1932. *The German Ideology.* www .marxists.org/archive/marx/works/1845/german-ideology/index.htm.

Marx, Karl and Engels, Friedrich. 1848. *The Communist Manifesto.* www .marxists.org/admin/books/manifesto/Manifesto.pdf.

McCabe, Herbert. 1987. 'Freedom' in *God Matters.* London, Geoffrey Chapman, pp. 10–24.

McCabe, Herbert. 2000. *The Teaching of the Catholic Church: A New Catechism of Christian Doctrine.* London, Darton, Longman & Todd.

McCabe, Herbert. 2002. 'The God of Truth' in *God Still Matters.* London, Continuum, pp. 29–35.

McLellan, David. 1972. *Marx before Marxism.* Harmondsworth, Pelican.

McLellan, David. 1973. *Karl Marx: His Life and Thought.* London, Macmillan.

Metz, Johann-Baptist. 2007. *Faith in History and Society: Toward a Practical Fundamental Theology.* Translated by J. Matthew Ashley. New York, Herder & Herder.

Miranda, José. 1974. *Marx and the Bible: A Critique of the Philosophy of Oppression.* London, SCM.

Neocleous, Mark. 2005. *The Monstrous and the Dead: Burke, Marx, Fascism.* Cardiff, University of Wales Press.

Rahner, Karl. 1978. *Foundations of Christian Faith: An Introduction to the Idea of Christianity.* Translated by William V. Dych. New York, Crossroad.

Ricœur, Paul. 1970. *Freud and Philosophy.* New Haven, Yale University Press.

Rose, Marika. 2023. *Theology for the End of the World.* London, SCM.

Schillebeeckx, Edward. 1963. *Christ the Sacrament of Encounter with God.* London, Sheed & Ward.

Schillebeeckx, Edward. 1987. *Jesus in Our Western Culture: Mysticism, Ethics and Politics.* Translated by John Bowden. London, SCM.

Scott, Peter. 2022. 'Theology After Marxism?' in Graeme Kirkpatrick, Peter McMylor and Simin Fadaee (eds.), *Marxism, Religion and Emancipatory Politics.* London, Palgrave Macmillan, pp. 39–57.

Strawson, Galen. 2004. 'Against Narrativity' in *Ratio: An International Journal of Analytic Philosophy* 17(4), pp. 428–52.

Surin, Kenneth. 1986. *Theology and the Problem of Evil.* Oxford, Wiley-Blackwell.

Tanner, Kathryn. 2004. *God and Creation in Christian Theology: Tyranny and Empowerment?* Minneapolis, Augsburg Fortress Press.

Turner, Denys. 1987. 'Feuerbach, Marx and Reductivism' in Brian Davies (ed.), *Language, Meaning and God: Essays in Honour of Herbert McCabe OP*. London, Geoffrey Chapman, pp. 92–103.

Turner, Denys. 2022. *Dante the Theologian*. Cambridge, Cambridge University Press.

Williams, Rowan. 2000. *On Christian Theology*. Oxford, Blackwell.

Yates, Stephen. 2017. *Between Death and Resurrection: A Critical Response to Recent Catholic Debate Concerning the Intermediate State*. London, Bloomsbury.

Acknowledgements

Grateful thanks to all those who provided comments on this Element, especially to Theodora Hawksley and James Lorenz, who provided commentary at a symposium on an early draft of the Element. Special thanks are due also to Tasia Scrutton.

In memory of Nahida and Samar

Cambridge Elements ☰

Christian Doctrine

Rachel Muers

University of Edinburgh

Rachel Muers is Professor of Divinity at the University of Edinburgh. Her publications include *Keeping God's Silence* (2004), *Living for the Future* (2008), and *Testimony: Quakerism and Theological Ethics* (2015). She is co-editor of *Ford's The Modern Theologians: An Introduction to Christian Theology Since 1918*, 4th edition (2024). She is a former president of the Society for the Study of Theology.

Ashley Cocksworth

University of Roehampton

Ashley Cocksworth is Reader in Theology and Practice at the University of Roehampton, UK. He is the author of *Karl Barth on Prayer*; *Prayer: A Guide for the Perplexed*; and (with David F. Ford) *Glorification and the Life of Faith*. His edited volumes include *T&T Clark Handbook of Christian Prayer*; *Karl Barth: Spiritual Writings*; and (with Rachel Muers), *Ford's The Modern Theologians: An Introduction to Christian Theology since 1918*.

Simeon Zahl

University of Cambridge

Simeon Zahl is Professor of Christian Theology at the University of Cambridge and a Fellow of Jesus College.

About the Series

Elements in Christian Doctrine brings creative and constructive thinking in the field of Christian doctrine to a global audience within and beyond the academy. The series demonstrates the vitality of Christian doctrine and its capacity to engage with contemporary questions.

Cambridge Elements ≡

Christian Doctrine

Elements in the Series

Life after Death after Marx
Simon Hewitt

A full series listing is available at: www.cambridge.org/ECDR

Printed in the United States
by Baker & Taylor Publisher Services